Praise for Black Son White Mother

Given South Africa's history of apartheid and racial oppression, in no other country is the issue of diversity more pronounced. Despite the hope and excitement during the birth of South Africa's democracy in 1994, almost three decades later we live in a country in which the dream of equality has remained elusive for the vast majority of Black South Africans. White South Africans have remained stuck in their ignorance and lack of knowledge of not only the lives of the majority black population, but also in their continuous denial of their white privilege. Likewise, Black South Africans have continued to be victims of a lack of diversity and equality in the workplace and society at large. At the macro level, it appears as if the quest for equality is only enshrined in the Constitution, while at micro level, inequality is experienced and perpetuated on a daily basis.

In *Black Son White Mother*, Charlie Masala and Gail Vermeulen have converted their personal experiences into an excellent work consisting of 22 easy-to-read chapters about the everyday reality of diversity in South African society. The reader is taken on a unique journey to unlock the potential of diversity in the workplace from the genesis of diversity in chapter 1 right through to embracing diversity in chapter 22.

The strength of the book lies in its practical wisdom expressed in succinct, yet profound pieces of insight and advice. You don't necessarily have to read it front to back (although I did so in only one morning). You can readily use it as a quick reference guide to find support for specific demands.

The book challenges and navigates the reader through some of the often unspoken realities of diversity, helping dispel some of the myths keeping you from transforming yourself in the space of ignorance or denial to setting yourself up for embracing diversity as a source of personal, business, and societal transformation.

When the South African Board for People Practices (SABPP) launched the world's first Employment Equity, Diversity, and Inclusion Standard in 2014, it was our hope that the standard would lead to South Africa's HR professionals rising to the occasion in internalizing diversity in their lives and work. Charlie and Gail are two such South Africans achieving exactly that with this seminal work on challenging our thinking and practices as we elevate our lived experiences into moments of personal and business empowerment in creating the diverse and equal society we dreamed about in 1994.

Marius Meyer
Chairperson: South African Board for People Practices (SABPP)
Program Leader in HR Management, Stellenbosch University

American Civil Rights Leader, Dr. Martin Luther King Jr., in his efforts to fight discrimination, gave a profound speech during the March on Washington for Jobs and Freedom on August 28, 1963, expressing his ultimate dream for civil and economic rights and an end to racism in the United States. He died for that dream. Nelson Mandela, the anti-apartheid activist, also fought for those who were disadvantaged by a system of racial segregation, and he went to the depths of prison for his conviction. It was a common cause that both these great men were prepared to die for. However, the human need and desire for social justice and equality will not be effectively attained until we all can see each other in our most naked and basic form – human (being).

My father, Dr. Myles Munroe, suggested that if we reduce people to human, we would realize that we are all the same – beautifully created by one God, under one creed, for one purpose, with varying potentials. Simply put, regardless of your skin color, race, socio-economic status, education level, gender, age, or disability, we are all interconnected with the inability to function alone. Value was intrinsic in our creation and essentially value is the very foundation that we as humans bring to each other (i.e. to employment) and need from each other. I am valuable, you are valuable, and together we bring greater value to our workplace, homes, schools, social life, and ultimately humanity.

Dr. Martin Luther King Jr. made a statement during his Nobel Peace Prize acceptance speech in 1964, "I believe that unarmed truth and unconditional love will have the final word in reality. This is why right, temporarily defeated, is stronger than evil triumphant."

We are looking for this "final word in reality" where the world is rid of all injustices and discrimination and where truth and love prevails; yet, we fail to recognize and implement the two greatest, if not only, ingredients necessary – understanding the love of God and the inevitable connection to one another. It's only when we recognize the intrinsic value in life based on our creator that we will see the value in our fellow human beings.

Charlie and Gail offer an eagle's eye view into what life has been for them during the ongoing fight for the truth and for love, and they have earned the right to put their stakes in the ground by providing great insight, principles, and wisdom in efforts to obtain real justice and peace in humanity.

Ms. Charisa Munroe-Wilborn
President: The Myles & Ruth Munroe Foundation
Vice President: Munroe Global Inc

From a South African perspective, the dreams and aspirations of a great nation anchored on the advantages of diversity can be traced back to the Congress of the People held in Kliptown as far back as 1955. This aspiration of a nation united in diversity is further affirmed in the preamble of our nation's Constitution, which boldly declares that "South Africa belongs to all who live in it, united in our diversity!" Yet, so many years since the dawn of democracy, the dream of a rainbow nation remains elusive as our country continues to struggle with the challenges of our diversified society through race, traditions, language, and culture. In present day South Africa, race relations have become so polarized that they threaten the very foundations of our young democracy.

As a result, this incredible book on diversity by Charlie Masala and Gail Vermeulen couldn't have come at a better time as its propositions offer impeccable solutions to managing and harnessing diversity for an inclusive and shared prosperity.

This book offers an unmatched and never-seen-before critical review of diversity challenges borrowing from the real life experiences of these two incredible authors, with Gail bringing the lens of a presumed beneficiary of the apartheid legacy experience, whilst Charlie brings the lens of a presumed victim of the ugly apartheid legacy. This unparalleled account of how to manage diversity in all sectors, be it civil society, public, or private sector, transcends the borders of South Africa. With these two authors being protégés of the late, world-renowned man of God, Dr. Myles Munroe, their work in this book acknowledges the challenges of diversities in a globalized world where organizations either have physical presences or their products are sold to customers across the world and where cross-border labor migration is a norm, resulting in organizations having to contend with multiple cultures, traditions, and religions.

This book could very well be key to a unity of the nations of the world and unimagined levels of commercial success and effective and efficient service delivery. I recommend this book as a toolkit for every supervisor, manager, or leader of an institution – big or small, private, civil, or public. A definite must-read!

Mr. Khathu Mike Ramukumba CA(SA)
MBA, Henley Businesss School
CEO: The Chemical Industries Education & Training Authority

Workforce diversity in modern times is one of the primary challenges for many businesses worldwide. Organizations need to recognize this awakening challenge and purposefully manage workforce diversity. Many articles have been written on this topic but this book is as authentic and practical as you can get. The vibrant authors and seasoned human resource practitioners of this book have managed to open up and focus on many countenances of workforce diversity: What is workforce diversity? What are the benefits of workforce diversity? What can leaders do to enhance workforce diversity? What are the disadvantages of workforce diversity? Workforce diversity is a complex phenomenon to manage in any organization. This book is well-crafted and a pragmatic tool to help increase organizational effectiveness, especially with current changes sweeping across the globe.

It is argued that organizations that value diversity will definitely cultivate success and have a future in this vigorous labor market. This book is therefore a must-read for all managers, leaders, and business owners in order to help recognize that increased mobility and interaction of people from diverse backgrounds as a result of improved economic and political systems, and the recognition of human rights, has put most organizations under pressure to embrace diversity in the workplace. Diversity brings with it the need to be nurtured, cultivated, and appreciated as a means of increasing organization effectiveness in this competitive world.

Francois Saunders
Retail Banking Executive
Bank of Gaborone, Botswana (member of Capricorn Investment Group)

❧◈☙

Diversity and inclusion is a global pandemic, and while it is a challenge, it brings a lot of opportunities. It brings diversity of thought, ideas, and perspectives.

In this book, *Black Son White Mother,* Charlie Masala and Gail Vermeulen challenge us to no longer be silent about matters of global interest like diversity and inclusion. It is the responsibility of all of us to rethink how we were socialized, and have diversity and inclusion discussions at family dinner tables.

We know that when we have corporates that embrace diversity and inclusion, they become profitable. It does not just become "the right thing" to do. I highly recommend this book to all leaders and managers across all industries.

Ms. Shirley Machaba
CEO: PwC South Africa
Southern Africa Regional Senior Partner, PwC

A lot of food for thought in a compact version. A valuable guideline for the aspiring executive, as well as replenishment of ammunition for the veteran leader.

Without diversity there would be no mutation in nature or progress in human society, which is part of this nature. I think this is the underlying concept addressed in this book. Well done!

Johannes Musel
Former CEO, Hitachi Power Africa

Whether we know it or not, we live in a diverse universe. The economy for doing business and building successful organizations is global. If we are not careful we can get stuck in our view of the world through the lenses of the local or national experience. The reason I am encouraging you to read, absorb, and put into practice the principles of *Black Son White Mother* is the authors' global experience. They have traveled to, studied in and gained knowledge from many other cultures and countries. This makes the value of this book priceless, because you don't have to travel to gain from their world experience.

The spirit of this book is very important at this time because, in my amazing country, the USA, we are taking advantage of timely opportunities to build on the principles of diversity.

Dr. Martin Williams
CEO: Martin Williams International,
Omaha-Nebraska,
USA

Charlie Masala and Gail Vermeulen capture in this book the very essence of what diversity means and the level of understanding and support needed to drive equality in the workplace. The approach of educating the public on what diversity is, and how it can cause people to behave deliberately and intentionally to oppress others or to simply ignore the needs of others, is clearly defined here.

They speak to behaviors that promote prejudice and beliefs that span years of ingrained and warped views on how people see others. This book lays the foundation for diversity by bringing to the forefront God's awesome creativity and imagination in the creation of his image in so many diverse images.

This book is not complicated or biased. It is simple and easy to understand. It is, without doubt, an awesome expansive insight into what needs to become a well-orchestrated journey of educating, raising awareness, adapting a strategy, and aligning people to purpose and process with a national vision that redefines who and what it means to be South African.

Mrs. Beverly Saunders
Vice President Training and Organization Development
Kerzner International
Atlantis, Paradise Island
Bahamas

This book is a must-read for government institutions and the corporate world. Charlie and Gail have ventured where eagles dare. Diversity cuts across all spheres of life. The 4th Industrial Revolution means that robots are taking over many tasks. We must use diversity to manage this collision between man and machines. Let's apply this book in real life situations and we will see change.

Mr. Kenny Mathivha
Spokesperson for Limpopo Premier
Government of South Africa

In this slim volume, Charlie Masala and Gail Vermeulen have given us a most insightful and incisive workbook on diversity and leadership in a fast-changing world. They begin with their own unique personal journey. Every transformation department and every diversity desk in the world should have a copy of this workbook.

Prof. Tinyiko Maluleke
Senior Research Fellow
University of Pretoria
Center for the Advancement of Scholarship

Praise for the Author Charlie Masala

I have known Charlie for over ten years. My father, Dr. Myles Munroe, was a mentor to him and he has been like a member of the family for quite some time. Charlie is a special and gifted individual who leads Munroe Global Africa as CEO, Board Member of The Myles and Ruth Munroe Foundation, and Regional Ambassador of The International Third World Leaders Association (ITWLA) for the SADC region of Africa.

Charlie is a go-getter. If you ever need someone on your team that just knows how to make the impossible happen, that person would be him. He has a calming spirit and is such a people person; I think this is his greatest trait. He knows how to motivate and empower people, not by force or manipulation but by being a servant leader and a man of compassion and empathy. His leadership has withstood many tests and I am happy to see that he has now chosen to share his knowledge and experiences by way of writing a book. His wisdom will definitely be a positive impact on anyone that is able to take hold of it and I am looking forward to being one of those who are impacted as well.

Myles Munroe Jr.
CEO: Munroe Global Inc
Chairman: International Third-World Leaders Association
Vice President: The Myles & Ruth Munroe Foundation

BLACK *Son* WHITE MOTHER

UNLEASHING THE POWER OF DIVERSITY IN THE WORKPLACE

CHARLIE MASALA
GAIL VERMEULEN

DEDICATION

Both authors of this book were mentees of late leadership expert from the Bahamas, Dr. Myles Munroe. He taught them invaluable lessons on what true leadership is about. Many books have been written on this very subject and a light bulb moment for them was when he said, "Get rid of all the different versions about leadership and remember two vital things, as true leadership is quite easy – it is about *inspiration* and *influence*."

As a senior manager responsible for transformation at the Office of the Auditor General, Gail Vermeulen extended an invitation to Dr. Munroe to address the organization the end of 1997. This was when Affirmation Action and Employment Equity had become focus areas for the government of South Africa as a post-apartheid measure to create social equity in the workplace. This was the first address to a South African company by Dr. Myles Munroe in corporate South Africa and the points he raised regarding diversity-related issues made everyone sit upright and reflect on their own lives and experiences.

This book is dedicated to a great leader who truly transformed lives as well as inspired those who attended the above address to think differently about the way people see each other and interact with each other from a behavioral perspective – both in the workplace and elsewhere. Many participants in the information session were so inspired by his truthful and direct address of the issues surrounding diversity that they shared with Charlie and Gail that, had they heard these wise words a long time ago, their lives would have been different. Some were even in tears as Dr. Myles called a spade a spade and didn't sugarcoat anything in his approach to diversity.

He emphasized the fact that all human beings, irrespective of race and gender, are equal in God's eyes and no one is inferior to anyone else. It is important to stand up and be counted, as your self-worth does not depend on others but comes from within you. He recounted an incident where a White schoolteacher had likened him as a Black person to a monkey, saying he would never achieve anything in life. This "truth" defined him! However, he made a conscious decision to prove his teacher wrong and went on to become a world-renowned leader. Many years later, Dr. Myles coincidentally bumped into that teacher who couldn't believe what he had achieved in life.

We therefore trust and hope that our mentor will be proud of this book dedicated to his legacy.

ACKNOWLEDGMENTS

By Charlie Masala

First and foremost, my thanks to my beloved wife of 17 years, *Xoli Masala*, who has stood by me and encouraged me to do God's will for my life. Secondly, to my children *Zoe, Okona,* and *Andisa-Makaria-Ruth* – thank you for allowing me to use my time, gifts, and talents to serve the world. My parents, *Wilson and Johanna Masala,* who raised me to understand, respect, and value human life, and embrace diversity.

Dr. Myles & Mom Ruth Munroe – you have been great mentors at an international level, exposing me to so much of what life has to offer, including my penning of this book. My beloved sister and brother, *Charisa Munroe-Wilborn and Myles Munroe Jr.,* for your continued support and relationship as we keep the legacy of our departed parents alive.

Mrs. Isabel Schonken, a white mother who discovered, trusted, and believed in me as a young man from a village in Venda, and ushered me into a great corporate environment, the Council for Scientific and Industrial Research (CSIR).

Mr. Victor Ramsingh, my HR Executive, for your support and love for me at the African Bank HR department.

Mrs. Linda Taylor, my White Aunt who moved into our area in 2010 after she lost her husband, Rob, in a robbery/shooting incident involving a Black man. Linda never held a stereotype against Blacks and we continue to learn from each other.

Mr. Bashiri Khan – my friend, you helped me overcome a stereotype I had held since childhood, as I was told and believed that all Indians were crooks. Through your friendship I experienced an honest Indian!

Mr. Frans Saunders – through your life and coaching I became a better professional. You were not just my boss in my job at African Bank but a brother, uncle, and father, who gave me knowledge and support as a mentor.

Mr. Joseph Khangale (Vho-Deze) – as I was growing up you taught me how to relate to adults as you were my older friend. You entrusted me with major responsibilities, including managing your transportation business and driving your truck as a teenager, serving the needs of our village.

Jerome Edmondson, my American brother who helped me fight some of my diversity battles with White South Africans with racist tendencies.

My Filipino friends, *Mr. Roy Oliveros and Lady Rochel Oliveros* – thanks for exposing me to the cuisines and culture of the people in the Philippines.

My Indonesian Mom, *Apostle Madam Indri Gautama* in Jakarta, Indonesia – thanks a lot for exposing me to Indonesia, the people, and culture.

Pastor Susan Kingal – thanks for inviting me to Papua New Guinea and exposing me to the PNG culture and kind people there.

Mr. Piet Motsweni – for walking a new path with me as we were both young and newcomers in the CSIR Human Resources Department where the two of us were literally the first Blacks to work in that historically Whites-only space!

My three former colleagues, *Cindy Mabaso (aka Sindisiwe The Prophetess), William Kasankola* and *Titi Sithole* – we were all in the workplace at a time when Blacks in professional appointments were still viewed as tokens by our White counterparts.

Dr. T.S. Muligwe, Bishop Solly Lalamani, Pastor George and *Mom Seny Mosena*, for your friendship and spiritual covering over the years.

Last but not least, I would like to thank my siblings: *Rudzani, Thomas, Norman, Linde, Job, and Unarine* – I am forever grateful for your love , support, and encouragement.

By Gail Vermeulen

My first acknowledgment goes to my parents, *Henry and Anne Fisher.* My father was a German-Jew who had to flee from Germany at the start of the Second World War and who by chance was put on a boat that took him to South Africa. Here he was forced to start a new beginning from scratch with very little money and without the rest of his family, who were shipped off to America. Coming from a very wealthy family in Germany, and having lost everything, he showed resilience and became the General Manager of the largest retail outlet in the Free State.

I need to thank my father for always giving me direction and sound advice, and for teaching me to always respect others – no matter their color or creed. He also taught me to always stand up for what I believe in.

My mother was much younger than my father. She came from a poor, conservative Afrikaans family, not Jewish but Dutch Reformed. This created a very diverse environment in which I was brought up.

My mother remains my role model as she led by example and always made people, no matter where they came from, feel special and at home. She related with ease both to our domestic worker and to the CEOs of companies that my father entertained at our home.

As a result of this upbringing that was by its very nature extremely diverse, it was natural for me not to look at a person's color, nationality, or race but rather at the person's character and heart.

Having worked in the corporate world at senior management/executive level the past twenty plus years, I was always nominated to lead the transformation initiatives and wish to thank the following people who positively impacted my life:

Shauket Fakie, former Auditor General of South Africa – He nominated me to lead the diversity initiatives and acknowledged my contribution. He was the first Muslim executive that I worked closely with and I was impressed with the manner in which he treated and trusted people.

Chris van Onselen, Regional General Manager, and *Michel Kircher,* Senior Manager Support Services from Sanlam – Thank you for teaching me to "go with the flow" and to be the "captain of my own ship."

Ian Patterson, CEO of Integrated Labor Solutions, who modeled the way for me to function at senior leadership level in a diverse team set-up.

Johannes Musel, former CEO of Hitachi – thank you for exposing me to different nationalities and to focus on the person and the competence of the person.

Pieter Kruger, Former Head of Legal at Mitsubishi Hitachi – he emphasized the importance of honesty and integrity, no matter the consequences.

Getty Simelane, former Head of HR at both Justin Avon and Deutsche Bank – the first black female in an executive position who inspired me and showed me that women need to be heard and that's okay.

Sweetness Malete, former Personal Assistant in Human Resources at African Bank, during my tenure as General Manager. She taught me that leadership comes from within yourself and encouraged me to change things and inspired me to do things differently, without fear.

Lastly, I need to thank my close family members for their unconditional love and support and for allowing me to be my authentic self. Above all, I need to thank *Dave,* my late husband of 38 years, for his patience and unselfish love.

All glory to God for crafting this incredible life journey for me and for the amazing, diverse people I have met along the way.

CONTENTS

FOREWORD

The Preamble to the Constitution of the Republic of South Africa recognizes the injustices of the past and gives recognition to and honors those who suffered for justice and freedom. It encourages all citizens to heal the divisions of our past and expresses the need to establish a society based on democratic values, social justice, and fundamental human rights.

The Constitution further enjoins all of us to be united in our diversity and despite all the challenges we have faced and continue to face as a nation, South Africans have a value system that refuses to die, which we call "ubuntu-botho." The word "ubuntu" is extracted from the word "umuntu" (for singular) and "bantu" (for plural) in isiZulu, which is in reference to a human being, and the word "motho" is a Setswana word for human being. In Setswana, the expression that represents an embodiment of humanity and great human values is "botho." Consequently, the expression is best articulated by using the idiom, "umuntu ngumuntu ngabantu" or "motho ke motho ka batho." Simply put, the expression literally means "a human being is a human being through others. I am because you are."

Ubuntu is a social construct premised on the notion of humanity and embracing diversity. It expresses a sense of communal capacity to show compassion, justice, dignity, and fairness among members of a community and broader society. It also expresses our inter-dependency and connectedness. It is through ubuntu that all human beings are able to find expression of their own sense of dignity, self-esteem, self-respect, and pride.

The first President of the democratic South Africa, Tata Nelson Mandela, will best be remembered, among other things, for being an evangelist for national reconciliation and non-racialism. To deepen this form of evangelism and his legacy, serious work is required to ensure every effort is made to avoid the return to the remnants of our horrific past, which was characterized by racial bigotry and hatred. In order to succeed in dismantling the legacy of apartheid, all of us bear the responsibility of working together towards an idea that it is still possible to see good in others. I would argue that there is no idea in the world that will ever gain traction without *discipleship*.

The book, *Black Son White Mother*, could have not come at a better time to carry forward that evangelism of deepening not only racial understanding and integration but ridding ourselves of ignorance about others and prejudice based on ethnicity, creed, class, and orientation in whatever form. The truth of the matter is that we are all part of God's creation and everyone is created with certain gifts, talents, rights, and responsibilities, and if we all learned to love more and judge less, this would be a better world and an oasis of hope.

I am unable as an individual to find true meaning and expression of my own humanity unless those around me are able to attain the same heights of exhilaration of human achievement and endeavor. Perhaps to put it in biblical terms, one can refer to the book of Proverbs: *"Do not withhold good from those to whom it is due, when it is in the power of your hand to do so"* (Prov 3:27 NKJV).

We thank Charlie Masala and Gail Vermeulen for reminding all of us of the need to embrace others and stay united in our diversity. This book is a useful tool and a rude awakening to all of us of the need to strive towards diversity. This is done throughout the book in a carefully balanced and responsible way that makes it easy to experience a paradigm shift in our idiosyncratic corners and gravitate towards the light of embracing diversity. It contains truth told in love and is a must-read for anyone who wishes to understand and see the value in others.

We are therefore being challenged to embrace a new and diversified way of thinking in our communities and in the workplace where we spend most of our precious time. It's time to think diversity in the workplace.

We congratulate the authors for being good disciples, forces of good in the world full of evil and for spreading this much-needed truth and evangelism!

Leslie Sedibe
Former CEO of the South African Football Association
Former CEO of Proudly South African
Admitted Attorney of the High Court of South Africa
Chairman: Leslie Sedibe Attorneys
BA, LLB, LLM (Tax) Wits University

PREFACE

The special relationship between
two people from diverse worlds

The two authors, Charlie Masala and Gail Vermeulen – Black Son White Mother – are the epitome of a diverse relationship that has gone way beyond that of the workplace. So where did it all begin?

Well, their paths first crossed in 1997 when Gail was appointed as the Human Resources and Transformation Manager at the Office of the Auditor General. She was interviewing candidates for vacant human resources positions and Charlie was a young graduate with very little experience. The panel decided to appoint some of the other candidates and discarded Charlie's application due to his lack of experience. However, Gail could not get this young black man out of her head due to the positive impression he had made on her. Yes, he had very little experience but his attitude and other attributes impressed upon her that here lay an uncut diamond – someone with immense potential. She therefore motivated for an additional position to be created specifically to assist her with transformation initiatives. Charlie was henceforth appointed and the journey began…

Gail took Charlie under her wing and showed him the ropes of a workplace, which was predominantly white. Together, they presented diversity workshops throughout the country to an audience of approximately 1200 people, also predominantly white. In the process of interacting on a daily basis with Charlie, Gail learnt many different lessons about diversity.

This young man demonstrated his ability to lead with humility, open-mindedness, and curiosity, and inspired Gail to learn and grow as much as he did. The relationship was based on trust, support, admiration, and learning, and both flourished!

Following her tenure at the Auditor General, Gail joined African Bank at a general management level and lo and behold recruited Charlie. He didn't hesitate to join her team. As a mother would look after her son, Gail made sure he was properly dressed in a time when he didn't have an abundance of money. This was important because Gail wanted to help him to be successful. She also heard all the interesting stories about girlfriends and when he met his beautiful wife Xoli he came to introduce her. Their journey continued and a working relationship turned into a special friendship such as that between mother and son.

When Gail turned 60 she asked Charlie to be the only speaker at this special occasion. Today, reflecting on this decision, she understands why. There is a very special bond between the two – spoken and unspoken. These two people from totally different backgrounds have accepted each other's differences, learnt about these differences from one another, and value and cherish them. They have both grown into the best versions of who they can be because of one another not despite one another. What was astounding for both of them to find out along the way was that despite their differences they both had the same values and attributes. They are both approachable people who relate to people of all ethnic groups and nationalities with ease. Both want the best for their children, and peace, harmony, and happiness. Both believe that honesty and integrity are key fundamentals for success. Both Charlie and Gail have been mentored by the same inspirational leader, Dr. Myles Munroe, and this helped shape their relationship and approach to life.

This diverse relationship has continued for more than thirty years, which shows that real diversity can not only work but can also create an intangible bond between two individuals who are so different yet so alike – like the bond between son and mother.

❧

Bridging our world's political and social divides is the challenge of understanding diversity. Charlie Masala and Gail Vermeulen have made a tremendous contribution to addressing diversity in corporate South Africa. One of these contributions is gaining understanding and practical knowledge of how diversity transforms all of our endeavors and how diversity in the realm of business and the workplace strengthens relationships and increases innovation and productivity when it is understood, managed, and celebrated.

The term diversity covers an array of differences – race, gender, class, ethnicity, sexuality, disability, religion, nationality – differences that have a deep impact on the very way people construct, assess, and interpret knowledge. Recognizing and supporting these interconnected differences have increased business, employee, and humanitarian success. Incorporating and promoting diversity throughout organizations at all levels is paramount in our continued and future success of humans on this planet. Continued transformation of our Private and Public Institutions will ultimately change the nation's climate as a whole.

From our experiences in the workplace it is clear that managers and leaders of organizations in South Africa do not know how to harness the positives that diversity brings and that they do not always see people as a source of competitive advantage.

In essence, leaders and managers do not understand the concept of diversity nor are they aware that employees do not only bring their expertise with them to the workplace but all their own baggage as well. In order to get them committed, managers and leaders must understand that "You can employ people's hands and heads, but their hearts they volunteer."

In short, the term diversity means "differences." A leader needs to understand that people are all different in the workplace and that the way one manages and leads them to achieve business results will to a large extent be based on a clear understanding and awareness of these differences.

Leaders and managers must be aware that diversity or differences will always be a challenge for them in the workplace but it is a reality, and if harnessed correctly can lead to a competitive business advantage. Diversity training, however, remains critical in the eradication of diversity illiteracy amongst leaders, managers, and staff.

Remember that "unity requires diversity but unity is not uniformity." Leaders and managers must inspire and influence people with differences to unite towards a common cause, that of business success, but within the framework of being themselves. Each person is unique and not a copy of someone else and that should be appreciated as such in the workplace. The fact that people do not think alike is a strength and not a weakness in the workplace and should be utilized for creative problem-solving within teams. "Alikeness" brings weakness, "Diversity" brings strength!

"All cultures are, good, bad, unique, dynamic, and sinful."
–Dr Elijah Maswanganyi, South African Pastor

Introduction

The year 2020 is a special but tragic time in the history of South Africa with the outbreak of the coronavirus pandemic. This has made us think more about the differences between people in this country but also about our similarities; it takes us back to the conversation we had with Dr. Myles Munroe regarding diversity in the workplace.

Firstly, COVID-19 highlights the differences between the living conditions of the rich and the poor, the different skill sets of the people of South Africa, the vast differences in religious beliefs, cultural background, ethnicity, race, and gender, different career paths and professions, and fields of expertise.

Secondly, it highlights the similarities between all these different groupings, as people want a similar outcome and the vast majority are prepared to stand together to achieve this. "Stronger Together" is the theme the South African government chose to get everyone to work together. The majority of South Africans want to survive this pandemic with minimum casualties and are striving for the same goals namely: health, peace, stability, security, having basic needs such as food, running water, electricity, and the ability to care for loved ones.

Thirdly, we have experienced true leadership from our president, the Honorable Cyril Ramaphosa, as he leads from the front inspiring and influencing a "rainbow nation" of people with a multitude of differences, to take hands and put these differences aside to defeat a common enemy – the invisible coronavirus. He leads as a true leader should with humbleness, dedication, open mindedness, and drive to achieve success for the country he clearly loves. His actions have inspired business South Africa and individuals with diverse interests to work together and put differences aside to defeat the invisible common enemy.

This difficult time in South Africa's history has taught us all that people with major differences can work together and be successful. This then begs the question of why since 1994 when South Africa became a democracy, are employers still battling to get this right in the workplace? Is it a lack of leadership, lack of awareness of what diversity really means, and an inability to harness it positively in the workplace, or what? If we look at the composition of the top structures in the workplace as well as at Boards of companies, the strength that diversity brings is not always reflected, despite legislative requirements such as Employment Equity and B-BBEE.

What a wasted opportunity for businesses in South Africa to fully capitalize on the positive opportunities and strengths that diversity can bring. If utilized and nurtured correctly, it can make a major difference to productivity and cohesion, and strengthen positive behaviors and mindsets in the workplace.

This book is written with the sole purpose of sharing lessons learnt along the way in a career of more than 20 plus years in the corporate world, and is based on the teachings and mentoring of leadership expert, Dr. Myles Munroe, as well as considerable international travel.

PART 1

THE DIVERSITY CONCEPT

1

THE GENESIS OF DIVERSITY

There are 7.8 billion people on earth today and it is amazing that no one has the same DNA coding or fingerprints, which explains how special every human is on the planet. Due to limited natural resources, humans are in a state of panic and are competing against instead of complimenting each other. All people on earth are created in the image and likeness of our creator, God, and we all therefore have the capacity to lead, create, and innovate. Never allow anyone's opinion of you to become your reality! People must learn that they were created different. "In diversity lies greatness." Throughout history, great achievements have happened despite humble beginnings.

The author of Diversity is the Creator of heaven and earth. When God created man he created both genders, male and female. When God created the earth with everything in it – trees, rivers, seas, mountains, and the animal kingdom with different types of animals. The lion, elephant, zebra, and leopard, for example, are all different in habits, looks, and survival instincts. Even in the jungle, no tree is the same and everything differs vastly. Together, this reflects the beauty of diversity! Furthermore, there is also night and day, as the world would not be able to function properly if there were only day or night.

God is a God of diversity

The human body itself is comprised of many different parts functioning differently but in harmony to achieve a common purpose – to make the whole body function. Each body part is unique and it is required for the effective functioning of the total human body.

It is important to note that God created "one man" from the ground and never went back to the ground to create another man. God created only one race called the human race and therefore our differences in skin color, color of our eyes, height, gender, or religious affiliation should not divide people.

- Unity is not uniformity or sameness.
- Unity requires diversity
- Differences are designed to accomplish a common goal where all efforts are appreciated
- Differences are necessary and essential
- Unity is distinctiveness going in the same direction to achieve a common purpose
- Unity in diversity is like an orchestra, where all the different musical instruments harmonize towards a common goal – a well-coordinated music piece in the ear of the listener

God does not expect people to be the same for the purpose of fitting in with others but rather to be unique and make their own contributions.

DIVERSITY DEFINED

From our experiences in the workplace, it is clear that managers and leaders of organizations in South Africa do not know how to harness the positives that diversity brings and that they do not always see people as a source of competitive advantage.

This is because they do not understand the concept of diversity nor are they aware that when you employ people they not only bring their expertise with them to the workplace but all their own baggage as well. In order to get them committed, managers and leaders must understand that "You can employ people's hands and heads, but their hearts they volunteer." This chapter deals with creating a clear understanding of what diversity really is.

People are different in so many ways – they come from different backgrounds, genders, education levels, careers, ethnic groups, race, sexual orientation, religion, wealth levels, belong to different communities, participate and support different sports, belong to different professional bodies, come from different societies, and have totally different personalities – all this within one country. Mix this with multinational companies where there are vast differences in thinking patterns and behaviors of people in the same workplace but from different countries in the world, then one can really talk about the "melting pot" that diversity brings to the workplace.

In short, the term diversity means "differences." A leader needs to understand that people are all different in the workplace and that the way one manages them to achieve business results will, to a large extent, be based on a clear understanding and awareness of these differences.

In order to harness the value of these differences to improve productivity and performance in the workplace, the manager or leader must be aware of these differences and know how to approach people differently to achieve the desired results. Isn't it true that for one person it is fine to be very directive towards and focus on facts whilst for another person it is more important to first inquire how the person is before giving the same facts to achieve the same results.

This is not rocket science, yet managers and leaders in the corporate world in South Africa and around the world still seem to be struggling with this.

Leaders and managers must be aware that diversity or differences will always be a challenge for them in the workplace, but it is a reality, and if harnessed correctly can lead to a competitive business advantage.

Remember that "unity requires diversity but unity is not uniformity." Leaders and managers must inspire and influence people with differences to unite towards a common cause – that of business success but within the framework of being themselves. Each person is unique and not a copy of someone else and that should be appreciated in the workplace. The fact that people do not think alike is a strength and not a weakness in the workplace and should be utilized for creative problem-solving within teams. "Alikeness" brings weakness, "Diversity" brings strength!

As is the case in the fight against the coronavirus, the country's leadership must use all strategies and possible measures for a positive outcome to maximize the positive impact that a diverse workforce can have on business results. Managers and leaders must have different strategies and tools that can be utilized.

Understanding the key dimensions of diversity in the workplace is the starting point, and as the decade progresses, these diversity dimensions may have sub-categories, such as age. Currently there are five generations in the workplace – Traditionalists, Baby Boomers, Generations X, Y and now Z.

14 DIMENSIONS OF DIVERSITY

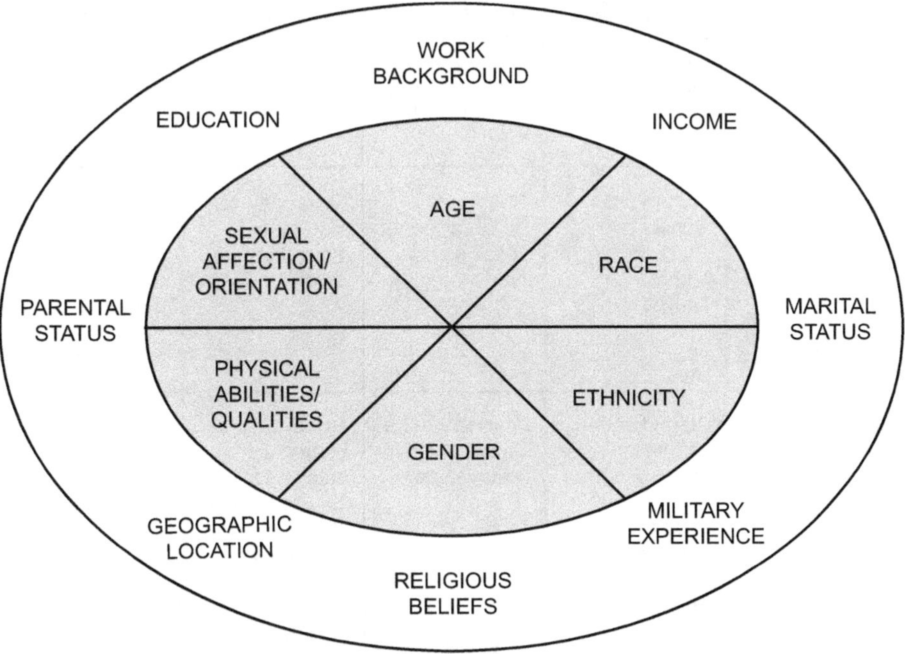

The following tables outline the different dimensions and messages that the authors of this book experienced. They illustrate the different worlds of the authors and the impact of diversity on future behaviors and decision making.

DIVERSITY DIMENSION – CHARLIE MASALA

Dimension	Detail	Messages Received	Impact	Lessons Learnt
Geographic Location	Rural upbringing Lived in same rural village in South Africa	Less opportunities in the village We followed Venda (Lemba Culture)	No knowledge of Urban South Africa Strong sense of domestic discipline	Clear understanding of the poverty and struggles of a rural upbringing No matter where you were born you can become a success
Parental Status	Venda (Lemba – Black Jew) speaking father and mother, married for 60 years	It is important to stay married once commitment is made, mother to be a homemaker	Commitment to a marriage is key no matter the differences	Wanted to pursue a career and support my family
Education	Rural Public School and Black Technikon/ University	Apartheid dictated "Bantu Black education"	Sister paid for my higher education studies	You can achieve anything YOU want to achieve and defeat poverty & apartheid
Work Background	Started at the bottom in Human Resources and worked myself up to become an International Speaker & Consultant	Important to be successful at what you do	Father was a boarding master, took care of college students. I wanted to be a supervisor/boss as I was growing up.	Hard work, commitment, and excellence are essential for success

Dimension	Detail	Messages Received	Impact	Lessons Learnt
Income	Low/no-class black family, father sole breadwinner, mother sew-ing clothes & making traditional beer	Only men should work whilst women must be home-makers	Determined to have a career and build a family	Poverty not funny therefore I should have an education to get a good job
Military Experience	No military Experience	Do not kill	No military experience but felt that military invasions based on defenseless and unarmed people is wrong	Avoid war at all costs, keep the peace
Religious Beliefs	Father & moth-er Christian	No freedom of choice	Religious people were always seen as trustworthy	No discrimina-tion of humans based on reli-gion. Kingdom of God is our goal.
Age	48 years (2020)	Matured man	With age comes wisdom, responsibility, and the ability to make a better world	The best is yet to come
Race	Black	Black = inferior & poor	We always started at the bottom, paid "black tax"	Apartheid a crime against humanity
Gender	Male	Males are head of the house/ home and every woman should listen not argue	Determination to start own family and change the narrative	Leading own home, empowering my three girls to be world leaders

Dimension	Detail	Messages Received	Impact	Lessons Learnt
Ethnicity	Venda (Lemba – Black Jew) & Zulu wife	Originally not acceptable to mix ethnicities	Ethnicity is important but must not control one's life	Accept other cultures, as good and bad is in all cultures
Physical Abilities	No disability	Keep healthy and exercise	Physically exercising & keeping fit	Better to build health than fight diseases
Sexual Orientation	Monogonous relationship	Taboo	Learn to accept people who are different from me	Don't discriminate against someone because of their sexual preference

DIVERSITY DIMENSION – GAIL VERMEULEN

Dimension	Detail	Messages Received	Impact	Lessons Learnt
Geographic Location	Urban upbringing Lived in different urban areas in South Africa, Free State, Western Cape and Gauteng	More opportunities in the city Free State, very Afrikaans, Western Cape socially superior, Gauteng economic hub of South Africa	No knowledge of rural South Africa Strengthened ability to adapt and built resilience to change	No clear understanding of the poverty and struggles of a rural upbringing No matter where you are you can find happiness and be successful
Parental Status	German/English -speaking father and Afrikaans mother married for 25 years	It is important to stay married once commitment is made and mother to be a homemaker	Commitment to a marriage is key no matter the differences	Wanted to pursue a career and be a homemaker – can do both

Dimension	Detail	Messages Received	Impact	Lessons Learnt
Education	English Public School and Afrikaans Universities	No money to send daughters for further studies, and seen as unnecessary	Determined to get a bursary for basic degree – BA Education and paid for my Honours & Masters	You can achieve anything YOU want to achieve
Work Background	Started at the bottom in Human Resources and worked myself up the corporate ladder to executive level	Important to be successful at what you do	Father was General Manager of a large retail outlet and I wanted to follow in his footsteps	Hard work and commitment are essential for success
Income	Middle class white family – father sole breadwinner	Only men should work whilst women must be homemakers	Determined to have a career and bring up a family (both)	Need to rise up and balance life in such a way to have a successful career and happy family
Military Experience	Father fled Germany as tanks arrived and Nazi regime took over	Don't let religion overpower your decisions	No military experience but felt that military invasions based on discriminatory influences are wrong	Discrimination destroys lives and takes away personal dignity
Religious Beliefs	Father was Jewish, Mother was Dutch Reformed. Neither religions prepared to accept the children in their religious domain	Freedom to choose own religion – Anglican church received children with open arms	Certain religions have ethnocentric beliefs	Ethnocentrism can cause destruction of lives

Dimension	Detail	Messages Received	Impact	Lessons Learnt
Age	62 years (2020)	Old and nothing more to add	With age comes wisdom and the ability to adapt	Age is just a number and there are many years ahead to make a difference
Race	White	Color makes no difference	Color blindness as color is irrelevant - it's about the person	Discrimination based solely on race is wrong
Gender	Female	Females should be home-makers	Determination to craft own career	Can successfully balance a career and family with extra effort
Ethnicity	Afrikaans and English	Both were acceptable	Ethnicity is important but must not control one's life	Be flexible and adaptable to all customs, which differ
Physical Abilities	Healthy with no disability	Take care of health, exercise	Did well in different sports	Sports allows for healthy competition
Sexual Orientation	Monogamous relationship	Accept different types of relationships	Mixed with gays and lesbians	Don't prejudge someone by their sexual preference as you will miss out
Marital Status	Parents married for 25 years despite diverse religions, nationalities, and languages	Respect differences and treat each other with dignity and without pre-judgment	Viewed differences as a positive	Diversity requires compromise and brings different perspectives

3

A SOUTH AFRICAN HISTORICAL PERSPECTIVE

I t is important for managers and leaders to be aware and understand the historical perspective of people that they manage in the workplace within the South African context. This is a unique context given the historical background of South Africa pre- and post the apartheid era. Apartheid was a political and social system in South Africa during the era of white minority rule. It enforced racial discrimination against Black Africans, mainly focused on skin color and facial features. The main reasons lay in ideas of racial superiority and fear. Across the world, racism is influenced by the idea that one race must be superior to another.

Apartheid called for the separate development of the different racial groups in South Africa. Apartheid made laws that forced the different racial groups to live separately and develop separately, and grossly unequally too. It tried to stop all inter-racial marriages and social integration between racial groups.

Apartheid has negatively affected the lives of all South African children and adults but its effects have been particularly devastating from a psychological point of view – badly affecting self-concept, self-worth, and self-esteem of the blacks who make up the majority of the population in South Africa.

The consequences of the apartheid era are still apparent today and also affect people who are currently employed in present day workplaces. Below are some key focus areas that have affected people due to this restrictive era in South Africa:

Firstly, job reservation – it is important to remember that certain jobs in South Africa where exclusively reserved for whites only as per apartheid government policy.

Secondly, the reservation of business rights – it is equally important to remember that certain businesses could only be run by White South Africans for a very long time.

Thirdly, pass laws – in South Africa prior to 1994 during the apartheid era there was a restriction placed on the movement of people.

Fourthly, there was an unequal education system – blacks were excluded from obtaining the same quality education as White South Africans.

Fifthly, there was forced segregation – the Group Areas Act kept people separated against their wishes.

Last but not least was the socio-economic circumstances in South Africa due to all the above-mentioned factors as well as others; there was a clear wealth distinction between the very rich and the very poor. This was sadly highlighted again during the coronavirus pandemic as the legacy of apartheid still reared its ugly head, highlighting its long lasting impact on wealth levels in South Africa where certain poor communities still do not have basic services such as decent housing, running water, and electricity.

Why should a manager and leader in the workplace be aware of this historical past? In a nutshell, it indicates and means that not all people in the workplace had the same opportunities to learn and develop and progress in careers. It also means that people in the workplace working together in a team or in one department have very little information and knowledge about each other and don't always understand the vast differences between ethnic groups, race, gender issues, and different socio-economic circumstances.

The challenge in the workplace that many managers and leaders face, is to clearly understand that it is not fair to "have a race in the workplace where people who have been in shackles for many years during the apartheid regime are required to run the same race as people who had been advantaged during the apartheid era." Obviously this race will become more equal post-1994 where The Constitution of the Republic of South Africa 1996 affords all South Africans equal access to schooling, housing, basic human needs, and the creation of equal opportunities for all in the workplace.

However, the legacy left by all the above factors mentioned in this chapter is still prevalent to those who have been left to deal with these issues. Remember, people bring their hearts and emotions into the workplace and not just their intellect and skills. Decades into South Africa's democracy, managers and leaders in the workplace still may be managing those left with these scars as it will take many decades to heal.

4

IMPACT OF CULTURAL PROGRAMMING

This then begs the question: "Where does cultural programming come from, as it seems to have a massive impact on our thinking process?" Well, it shapes our thinking and we bring this into the workplace and into our daily interactions with people who are similar and also different to us.

"Cultural programming" is messages received from the various dimensions of our lives from childhood right through to adulthood. This conditions us to see the world in a very specific way. This is reinforced by the major players in our life and becomes ingrained in our thinking process through constant reinforcement.

The most important are the messages we received from our parents, relatives, families, and communities about other people and how they perceived them.

These messages also come from and are reinforced throughout our lives by our religious beliefs, the type of education we receive, the type of work or profession we have chosen, professional organizations we belong to, and our specific race, gender or ethnic group. Traditions in different race and religious groups regarding key occasions such as births, weddings, funerals, day to day interactions, and sports activities can differ vastly. These are just some of the key focus areas of cultural programming and this is by no means a finite list, as there are too many to mention.

Because of the history of South Africa, groups of people have been kept at a distance from one another, resulting in limited socialization and thereby limiting our experiences of one another. Lack of knowledge of each other's traditions, religious beliefs, and ceremonies has reinforced our own cultural programming.

It is important to remember how strong this programming is and that managers and leaders as well as team members bring these preconceived ideas to the workplace. It is a fact that it is not only the person and his/her mental capabilities that comes to work, but the whole person with all his/her thoughts – both head and heart.

Therefore, the challenge in the workplace is to understand the long-lasting effects that cultural programming has on all people and to ensure that diversity in itself does not become a barrier to managers and leaders but rather a strength. Remember, differences are normal and have and will always be there, so change your attitude to diversity and view and use it positively!

Managers and leaders must understand the cultural programming their workforce has been subjected to, and more importantly, understand where their own cultural programming comes from in order to understand how their judgment calls, behavior, and thinking processes have been influenced. This will positively or negatively impact the way they lead and manage diversity in the workplace.

A clear self-awareness of cultural programming is crucial if managers and leaders are to embrace the viewpoint that people are a source of competitive advantage in the business environment.

CULTURAL PROGRAMMING

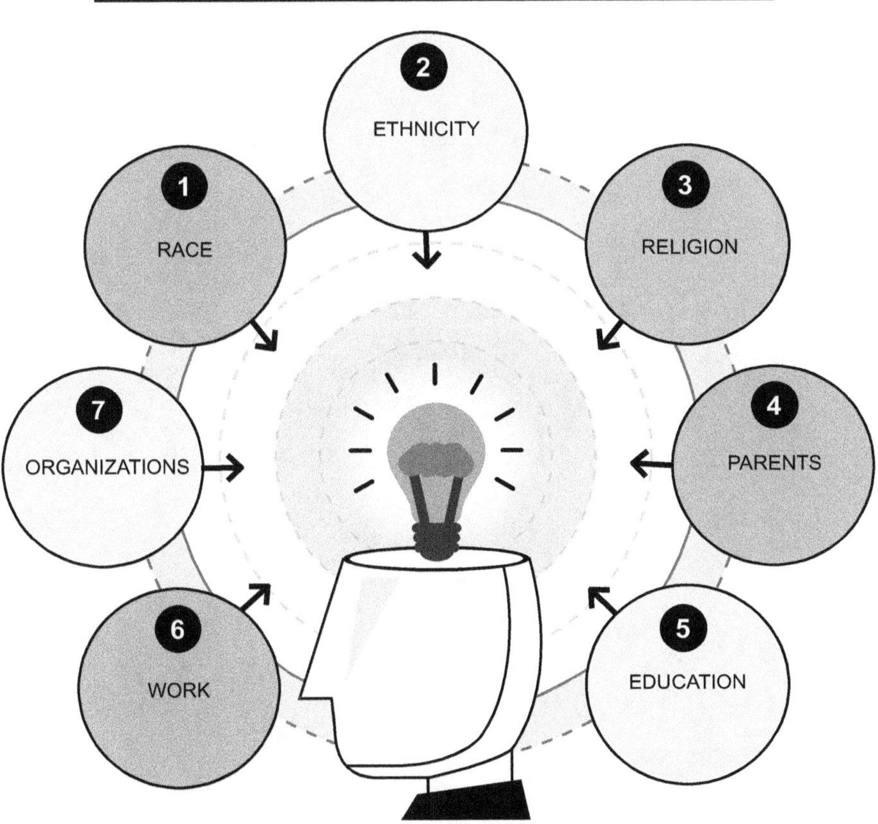

The above diagram illustrates some of the key sources of cultural programming that have informed our behaviors and way of thinking. This is not a finite list but it highlights the sources of key messages received and which of these impact most on people in the workplace.

PART 2

PURPOSE, CHALLENGES, IMPACT AND POWER OF DIVERSITY

5

THE CHALLENGE OF DIVERSITY IN THE WORKPLACE

Now that we all understand what diversity means we also need to understand that the problem in the workplace is not diversity per se, but it is our *attitude* towards diversity that causes problems. People who have negative attitudes towards other people's differences often engage in behaviors that negate the positive benefits resulting from differences in the workplace. So, what are some of these behaviors and attitudes?

Well, many leaders and managers can be biased, can stereotype and even discriminate against those people in the workplace who are different to them. The tragedy is that they are probably not even aware they are doing this.

The only way to solve this problem is to *create awareness*. Managers and leaders must be aware of their own attitudes towards diversi-

57

ty-related matters, as their attitudes will influence their behaviors in a negative or positive manner. This in turn will either promote positive teamwork and increase productivity and business results and promote constructive workplace relationships, or have the opposite effect – increased conflict in the workplace and a lesser focus on productivity and good business results.

The people in the team or within the department will take their cues from their manager or leader, thereby reinforcing outdated behaviors or replicating constructive business attitudes and behaviors.

So... change your attitude to a positive one!

Attitude is the master key to your success – it will open or close doors for you. We have seen managers and leaders not being promoted in the workplace – not due to their skills but their attitudes. People who are resilient to change and adapt to survive changes also have the ability to change their attitudes. Teaching skills to a positive person is easy but it is more difficult to teach a skillful person to change their attitudes.

The management and leadership challenge in a diverse work environment is to ensure that people change their attitudes to see diversity in a positive light – diversity should be viewed as a strength not a weakness.

Former American President, Theodore Roosevelt, reminded us that the most important single ingredient in the formula for success is *knowing how to get along with people*. Those who have positive attitudes in the workplace and who have the skills to match are more likely to be successful and get promoted. The promotion per se did not give the person a good attitude but an outstanding attitude resulted in the person being seen as a high achiever.

6

LEADERSHIP IS NOT EXCLUSIVELY RESERVED

As managers and leaders we believe that we are the superior ones and the only leaders in the workplace. This comes from our own philosophies that say we love and cherish our own thoughts and values. But a manager and leader who understands and accepts the power that diversity brings to the workplace will understand that being an exclusive leader excludes others who can also lead but from a different place.

Share the leadership role by embracing the idea that:

- Trapped in every person in your team is a hidden leader.
- Every human was created to lead and designed for dominion.
- Leadership potential resides in every individual.
- In every team member there is a manager and a leader in the making.

- True leadership is self-manifestation with due care for others who are different from me.

As true leadership is about inspiration and influence, ensure that you as senior managers and leaders empower others to also lead, resulting in growth and development and not stagnation. Unleash the hidden talent of others and you may be surprised at how much you as a manager and leader will learn.

They say there are three types of managers and leaders:

- Those who make things happen
- Those who see things happen
- Those who wonder what happened

Your task as a manager and leader is to ensure that because you understand the value and strength that diversity brings, you go out of your way to "push people out of their comfort zones where they are happy but where there is very little growth." It is your job to ensure that you care enough for your people to mentor and coach them to become comfortable with being leaders in their own sphere of influence.

Be a Leader Generator and unleash the potential in current and future leaders!

7

SELF-AWARENESS AS A DIVERSITY LEADER

As a manager and leader, *you* may be the barrier to diversity impacting positively on your business results. If this is true then you need to have the courage to remove yourself as this barrier, and *change.*

The key questions you need to ask yourself to establish if you are a barrier and stumbling block are the following:

- Do you understand that diversity itself isn't a problem – it can add value to organizations?
- Do you understand that our differences have always been there and they are what make us unique?
- Do you understand and accept that the problem is not diversity per se but lies in our attitudes towards diversity?
- Do you understand and acknowledge that people who have

negative attitudes towards other people's differences often engage in behaviors that are stereotypical, prejudicial, and discriminatory?

Get out of your own comfort zone, *be a diversity champion* and let yourself learn and grow. Confront your own skeletons in your closet and have a tough conversation with yourself regarding the main barriers to diversity, which are:

- Ethnocentrism – do you still think you are superior to others?
- Prejudice – due to your cultural programming are you biased towards some people?
- Stereotyping – do you take your bias and pull it across a whole group of people?
- Discrimination – do you treat people who are different to you according to their differences?
- Racism – do you still think your race is superior to others?
- Attitude – do you have a negative attitude towards diversity adding value in the workplace?

If you answer yes to any of the above questions you are a close-minded manager and leader and will never be open to accepting the fact that in diversity lies strength which will improve business results. *You* are the barrier, so move out of your comfort zone and grow!

Diversity-illiterate leaders and managers are usually contributors to a workplace where diversity is not celebrated nor tolerated. Managers and leaders who are the barriers in the workplace can consider the following lessons learnt from a teaching environment:

Students don't fail a class because they can't learn but because the teacher can't teach! Astute managers and leaders will therefore use diversity to positively impact on improved business productivity by not allowing their own cultural programming to stand in the way. After all, the main role for managers and leaders is to focus on how to improve business results. Therefore, get the job done by harnessing the power that diversity brings as a business tool to improve workplace productivity.

Be a courageous manager/leader and diversity champion and take the self-appraisal below:

- Are you aware of your ethnocentric beliefs, behaviors, stereotyping, and prejudices?
- Have you created a greater understanding of yourself?
- Have you developed good working relationships with those who are different as well as similar to yourself?
- Have you succeeded in creating effective work teams with diverse team members?
- Have you created improved customer/client service satisfaction?

As a manager and leader who clearly understands and supports any form of diversity in the workplace, be ahead of others and allow diversity to impact positively on improved productivity!

DIVERSITY IS THE SUM OF

D	=	DIFFERENCES ADD VALUE
I	=	INDIVIDUALITY IS A GIFT
V	=	VALUE DIFFERENCES
E	=	EQUALITY IS A BIRTHRIGHT
R	=	RESPECT THE VIEWS OF OTHERS
S	=	SUCCESSFUL BUSINESS TOOL
I	=	INFLUENCE OTHERS
T	=	TRUST IS THE FOUNDATION FOR SUCCESS
Y	=	YES, YOU CAN CHANGE AND LEAD

8

ETHNOCENTRISM

Whether we like it or not we all have our own belief system and we all bring this to the workplace. As a manager and leader have you ever heard of the term "Ethnocentrism"? A fancy word but a crucial one in coming to a clear understanding of how your belief system influences your behavior as a manager of people in the workplace. So what does this mean and how does it work?

Ethnocentrism is a belief in the inherent superiority of one's own group or culture, accompanied by a feeling of contempt towards other groups and their cultures i.e. the way they do things. This means that you as a manager and leader see things through rose-tinted glasses and subconsciously decide that anything that is different from your way of thinking, your views and behaviors is seen as not good and acceptable as it is substandard.

When you apply this thinking to unimportant issues such as the brand of your toothpaste or the BMW that you drive and think that no other car can be in the same class, it is harmless. The problem comes in when you think in this manner about *important issues* that affect the lives of those people you manage or lead.

As a manager and leader you may think that females can never be as good as males to lead others or that younger professionals can never contribute as much as older professionals or that your religious and cultural beliefs are the only ones that are acceptable and are right.

This type of thinking will alienate you from managing and leading your people and harnessing their true worth in the workplace. For example, younger professionals bring different perspectives than older workers to the workplace – a different and fresh way of thinking and tackling of problems. The lesson that managers and leaders should learn is that it is normal to like or even prefer to be with people who are similar to themselves. This could be due to various factors such as it is familiar or it makes one feel comfortable. Managers and leaders must be aware of this thinking process as it can distort one's thinking. The danger is that it can be a source of prejudice, bias, stereotyping, and even discrimination in the workplace.

Remember that ethnocentrism is often not based on true facts. The fact that one thinks that BMW is the only car to drive may not be the sole truth. Mercedes or Audi can be just as good. When one then applies this type of thinking to more important matters such as religion, cultural traditions, age, race, gender, or persons with a disability in the workplace, it can distort the true or real picture, and your behavior towards those people will be in line with this type of thinking.

A distortion of the truth and real facts… so be aware and be careful! Ethnocentric beliefs can have a far-reaching impact on your life and your work.

PITFALLS OF ETHNOCENTRISM

Let's take a snapshot of this impact:

1. Decisions are made based on unrealistic comparisons

The attitude of ethnocentrism is always one of *superiority*. Someone from outside of an existing culture is judging the actions of other people based on perspectives gained without the use of wisdom. Although every person on our planet has their own definition of "normal," we cannot apply this observation to everyone else. Each person, even within a similar culture or ethnicity, leads an independent life. Their perspectives and differences are unique.

This means the conclusions which people draw when using ethnocentrism as their foundation for decision-making are based on generalizations and opinions instead of *facts*. Because this information does not include the other side of the equation, the conclusions we reach when using this approach are misleading at best.

2. Ethnocentrism can cause societal polarization

It is easier to be scared of something or someone who is different from you than it is to embrace the diversity that can develop through the intermingling of ideas. When we think of someone who comes from a different culture, then the initial perspective tends to be one that looks at what we don't like about that other system. Ethnocentrism is an embrace of negativity because the only goal of this approach is to prove individualized superiority. It makes us feel good to think that the decisions we make in life are better than the ones that other people make, especially in the areas of religious salvation, moral fortitude, and family planning.

When you have two individuals or groups who look at each other and think that the other culture is inferior to theirs, then you create polarization in society. With each group not willing to compromise because they fear there is a lack of morality or superiority, then people take sides instead of trying to get along with each other.

3. It can impact every aspect of life if we allow it to do so

People can separate themselves even in the same religion by preferring one denomination over another because they think their belief structure is the best one to follow. Any time we think of one group as being superior to another (and that we are in that superior group), then it isn't an ego talking but the philosophy of ethnocentrism rearing its ugly head.

This belief system requires us to close off our minds to different perspectives and opinions. We can no longer choose to believe anything but our own thoughts or ideas because no one else can be correct. That is why societies self-destruct over time – because no one is willing to listen to what anyone else has to say. Life becomes more about what is said in the echo chamber instead of outside of it.

4. Ethnocentrism drives people away from what they love

If the only thing a person experiences in life is rejection, then there is no desire to be around people who think of them as being inferior. This attitude drives a wedge between groups where those who are in the minority often feel like the only option available to them is to leave. Communities in the United States are becoming more like-minded than ever before because of this very reason. The recent "Black Lives Matter" campaign, which has caused a worldwide reaction, is one key example of this. Whenever the approach of ethnocentrism is taken, it creates a circumstance where individuals or groups give each other ultimatums.

5. It is a philosophy which limits the human perspective

Have you ever seen someone resist change even though the new policies or procedures they were being asked to follow would make life easier? That is another example of ethnocentrism at work. Just because someone has been completing the same task in the same way for a long time doesn't mean that it is the best way to operate. The act of dismissing any thought of evolution or change at the micro or macro level is evidence of an ethnocentric perspective.

6. Ethnocentrism can have deadly results

Are you the type of person who gets angry when someone has a disagreement on an opinion you have shared? The problem that ethnocentrism ultimately brings to humanity is its nature of escalation. People become blinded by their personal perspectives to the extent where it becomes the correct choice for them to enforce their philosophies on other people at any cost.

7. This philosophy can create isolation

Some people like to be by themselves for personal reasons but ethnocentrism can cause social isolation simply because someone feels different (and superior) to everyone else. Even small groups of like-minded people who do not experience diversity in thought or opinion can experience this disadvantage together. There is boredom when you are around the same people all of the time with limited sources of entertainment.

8. Ethnocentrism limits the choices people can make

When you only respect and accept your own grouping, you hinder or limit your choices.

9. Ethnocentrism hinders the work of cultural assimilation

When one only focuses on your own culture, you lose out on the golden opportunity to learn about other cultures.

FROM ETHNOCENTRISM, PREJUDICE, & STEREOTYPES TO PRODUCTIVITY

Awareness of our ethnocentric beliefs, behaviors, stereotypes, & prejudices

Greater understanding of self

Developing effective work relationships with those who are different, as well as similar

Effective teamwork & customers

Greater productivity

9

THE POWER OF PREJUDICE

So what then is prejudice and how does it impact on people in the workplace? Prejudice is a *preconceived feeing or bias*. It is when one makes an opinion or makes a judgment call about someone but without the true facts.

It is important to note and be aware that as long as biases are about unimportant things or issues then this is relatively harmless. However, where managers and leaders hold prejudices against certain people in the team, it can be dangerous. Due to this type of thinking the manager and leader can limit career development and progression as opportunities to develop will most likely be limited.

If you are prejudiced about the brand of your toothpaste and think that it is the only correct brand then that's fine. But if you are biased towards people who have children because you don't want children, then you will never treat them as equals in the workplace nor have empathy for the challenges faced by working mothers and also not consider flexibility of any kind for them in the workplace.

Managers and leaders must be aware that they bring their prejudices/biases to the workplace and more importantly that they come from their own cultural programming, as already discussed in the book.

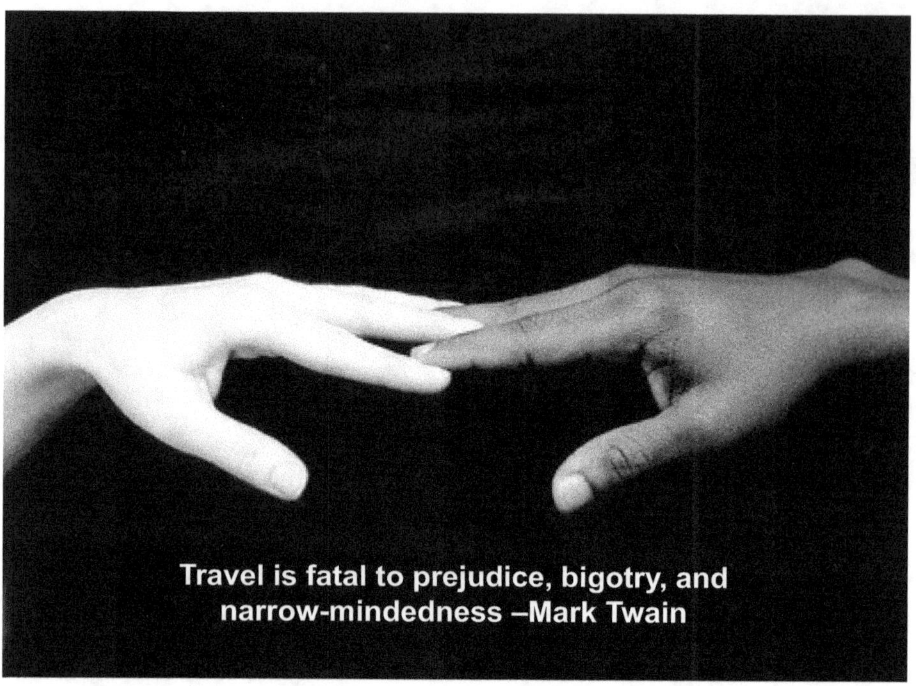

10

THE DANGER OF STEREOTYPING

What must we know about stereotyping and its impact on managers and leaders in the workplace? Stereotyping is when we apply our prejudices/biases to all members of a specific group of people. Some examples are: all blacks are lazy, all whites are rich and racist, all blondes are dumb, all coloreds are drunkards, all young professionals are entitled and think they have all the answers, and people with disabilities are not intelligent.

This way of thinking also comes from our own cultural programming. The danger of stereotyping is that the person whose thinking is distorted will spread this to others in the workplace and it will impact on their behavior towards other people.

As a manager and leader you might have had a black person to manage and that person was lazy therefore the next black person in the team will be seen as lazy as well. This will impact on the manner in which you will manage that person and will probably lead you to micromanage the new person. This person in turn will feel uncomfortable as your micro-managing of a high performing individual is unwarranted and based solely on your stereotyping. This person will then most likely leave the company and at the same time reinforce your own stereotype that all black people are lazy and cannot meet the high standards set by the company.

Stereotyping is dangerous in the workplace as it leads to assumptions that are not supported by facts and may be offensive and even destroy or limit people's careers, thereby not unleashing their potential.

Sometimes the chains that prevent managers and leaders from being free are more mental than physical due to their own cultural programming.

Be careful not to reinforce distorted thinking across groups of people you manage and lead, as valuable people may be lost to the company – they either leave or become totally disengaged!

11

THE SIN OF DISCRIMINATION

Our distorted way of thinking may even lead to discrimination in the workplace. This happens when managers and leaders treat people in the workplace in a negative manner. As a manager and leader from a specific race, gender, and age group, one may have people in your team who are from a similar background therefore one gives them the challenging work and speaks informally to these persons in order to get to know them better – this is familiar! Conversely, those who are most different to the manager or leader are kept at a distance and given routine tasks, limiting their development and minimizing personal contact – this is uncomfortable to the manager and leader!

What a tragedy and how dangerous is this in the workplace! The manager and leader may be missing out on developing the most competent people in their team and spending time on those who have the least potential to be successful based solely on ignorance and distorted thinking. This supports the fact that South Africa has made little progress since 1994 in terms of representivity on senior/executive and Board levels of those disadvantaged by the apartheid era in South Africa (Department of Labor, 2019). We still have the "Irish coffee syndrome – white at the top and black at the bottom."

Discrimination can still be observed in the workplace of today where women are paid less than their male counterparts doing the same job, and lack of female representation on senior executive levels. Similarly, people of a certain race group, gender, or religion are promoted solely based on the aforementioned factors and not necessarily on competence.

Discrimination in the workplace also negates the constitutional right of an equitable workplace for all.

Remember, discrimination is done in subtle ways so as not to draw too much attention – it is systemic/ingrained in nature and this is where the danger lies!

The "concrete wall" and "glass ceiling" for women in senior management and executive positions, as discussed in *Our Separate Ways* by Ella Bell and Stella Nkomo, illustrates the challenges that women still face in the workplace today:

- Doses of Racism and Sexism – women are not always taken seriously
- Proving Your Competence – women need to work twice as hard to be recognized
- Invisibility Vice – women are heard but not listened to
- Challenges to Authority – different viewpoints are not easily accepted
- Stereotyping – women are emotional and not factual

- Exclusion from the Old Boys Club – women are not seen as equals and are therefore excluded
- Sexual Static – women are mainly viewed as sexual objects
- Self-Limiting Behaviors – behaviors of women are highlighted as self-limiting

The analogy between the management and leadership of the COVID-19 pandemic in South Africa in 2020, and how we manage diversity-related matters in the workplace, highlights the following:

- Just as the coronavirus does not discriminate on the grounds of gender, race, or wealth levels, so we too should not discriminate on any arbitrary grounds in the workplace by striving to create an equitable workplace for all.
- Just as the coronavirus has all South Africans focused on how to minimize the risk of an unknown invisible common enemy by standing together, so too should we focus all the efforts of all our employees in the workplace, no matter how diverse, towards the achievement of business results.
- The slogan of "Stronger Together" should be embraced and harnessed in the workplace as during the management of the coronavirus in South Africa in 2020.
- Let's embrace differences as it is these differences that make South Africa unique and that should give us the competitive advantage to deal with challenges. This is similar to the manner in which different skill sets and viewpoints have been used and considered in the fight against COVID-19 in 2020.
- The generosity of all South Africans to contribute money, time, and skills to others, no matter how much or how small in this time of crisis, should be an example of how the true spirit of "Ubuntu" that is unique to South Africa can set the

manner in which managers and leaders in the workplace should embrace diversity and see it not as a barrier but a distinct advantage.

12

THE UNACCEPTABILITY OF RACISM

Sometimes people say, "I don't see color" but that doesn't always ring true! This may indicate the hiding of true beliefs and that one is in denial. One cannot embrace and accept something that is not visible. A black man remains black and a white woman remains white!

Furthermore, this denial may indicate an unwillingness to accept that South Africa has different races who are all equal and have to work together.

During the apartheid era, color was the main basis to discriminate against and segregate a people group. A denial of seeing color negates the ability to reverse the discrimination of the past.

You need to see color in order to consciously deal with the effects of apartheid and to embrace diversity.

Racism is a belief system that one race is superior to another and has the right to dominate. Racism is recognized worldwide as a crime against humanity as it dehumanizes people.

Embracing diversity therefore means you see color, accept color, and are willing to accept people for who they are.

PART 3

MAXIMIZING DIVERSITY IN BUSINESS AND WORKPLACE

13

THE BUSINESS CASE OF MANAGING DIVERSITY AND ECONOMIC INCLUSION

In the United States, they talk about diversity and the inclusion of minority-owned businesses. In South Africa, we call this Broad Based Black Economic Empowerment (B-BBEE). This is inclusion of the previously disadvantaged Black majority of the population. The Department of Trade and Industry outlined and legislated the five pillars of B-BBEE to redress the past injustices of apartheid, namely:

1. Ownership by previously-disadvantaged groups
2. Skills Development
3. Enterprise Development
4. Socio-Economic Development
5. Employment Equity

We have entered a historic convergence of the 14 major areas of change affecting business and the workplace. These areas are complex and usher in a new era of managing diversity – both nationally and globally. They are as follows:

1. Technological explosion for industrialization
2. Globalization (the coronavirus pandemic), which has impacted our lives, business, and travel – probably forever.
3. Economic trade wars and clashes (more visible between the new two superpowers, China and the United States of America)
4. Religious confusion
5. Global institutions making demands for change of cultural practices taking away national sovereignty
6. Digital explosion in the Information Communication Technology (ICT) sector and introduction of 5G technology
7. Political transition (from national politics to world dominance, billionaires taking center stage in politics)
8. Rapid transformation
9. Longevity in life expectancy (due to medical advancements)
10. Global merger/takeover strategies of mega industries
11. Decolonization
12. Business technology advancement due to the 4th Industrial Revolution
13. Global fear and mistrust
14. Re-colonization (not just political but economic this time around)

Unprecedented, and on an international scale, most countries in the world are sharing information and pooling resources to find a cure for a common enemy threatening the survival of all people – the coronavirus. Hopefully a vaccine will shortly be forthcoming under the guidance of the World Health Organization.

Given all these factors, the crucial question is then what gets priority in your own workplace – your own cultural programming or what the business expects in order to secure one's own economic survival?

In the real world of work, managers and leaders need to understand that they must be aware of cultural differences and programming but at the same time balance this with the needs of the business.

Where one's programming is in conflict with the values, policies, and procedures of the company, then the values of the company will take precedence. An example is, "I believe in African time and therefore always come late for meetings." As a manager and leader, this is a good opportunity to understand that this viewpoint is due to cultural programming. As a leader, one is then expected to explain the business reason of why the person should be on time for meetings and the effect that coming late has on other people in the meeting and that people may feel disrespected. Furthermore, the leader must ensure that business outcomes are achieved and that this requires everyone's full inputs.

Where companies can be flexible to accommodate time off for traditions due to cultural programming such as funerals, weddings, and religious ceremonies, make that happen! This must, however, always be done within the confines of consistency and fairness to all employees.

A good example is a Muslim employee asking to leave earlier during Ramadan due to fasting requirements. If this is operationally possible, be flexible and ensure that this employee works in the hours taken off at a later stage. More importantly, communicate your decision to all people in your team. This creates greater understanding of why you as a manager and leader are granting this exception and it also fosters appreciation for differences.

So, as a manager and leader, you are tasked with the challenge of achieving business results through people who are diverse and will require open and honest communication and flexibility. Never at the cost of achieving the desired business results! You need to see color in order to consciously deal with the effects of apartheid and to embrace diversity.

14

THE IMPACT OF LOW EXPECTATIONS

So, if you as a manager or leader, due to your own cultural program-ming, have low expectations of a person reporting to you, then what generally happens in the workplace?

Based on the manager's own prejudices, if he/she thinks that a person cannot do the job, then the following normally transpires:

- The manager or leader distrusts the person because he/she doubts that the person will deliver on expectations, resulting in micro-management and over-control, causing the manager to show an autocratic management style towards this person.

- The manager will minimize social interaction with this person in the workplace and stop listening to any inputs they can offer on work-related issues.

- The person on the receiving end of the manager's behavior

will see and feel this isolation and start to harbor resentment towards the manager. This then reinforces the over-controlling actions of the manager, creating more uncertainty for the person on the receiving end who consequently shows a non-caring attitude and total apathy towards his/her work.

- The end result is that the person will fail and will not develop his/her potential and will speak to everyone about what is happening, except taking the matter up with the manager due to a relationship of distrust.

- This behavior then confirms the prejudice/bias of the manager that "I was right about this person." This person was not productive, did not perform as expected.

- The circle of prejudice towards the person based on preconceived bias/ideas about this person is reinforced and strengthened.

- The person on the receiving end will most likely leave the company with their own prejudice about the manager, for example "all white female managers are autocratic and over-controlling."

- The manager will be hesitant to appoint a similar person again as all young black professionals are overrated and lazy.

- This is a lose-lose situation in the workplace for the company, manager, and employee.

- Furthermore, in the South African social context, these workplace experiences have strengthened prejudices for all parties concerned but in a negative way and will be communicated to others as such.

HOW LOW EXPECTATIONS AND PREJUDICE AFFECT PERFORMANCE

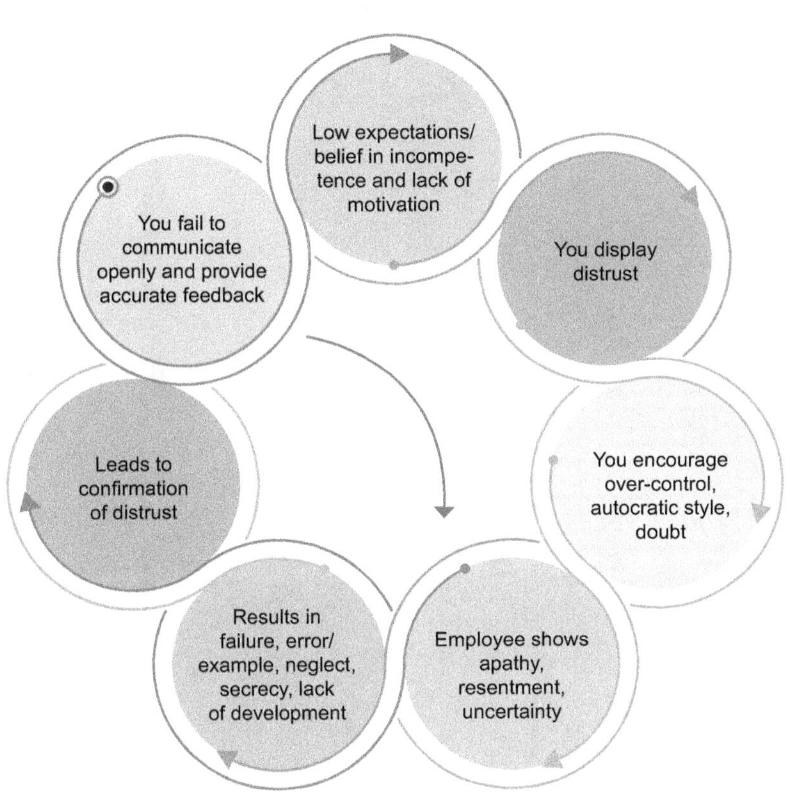

15

THE IMPACT OF HIGH EXPECTATIONS

Conversely, where a manager or leader believes that a person will succeed in the workplace due to the manager's or leader's own belief system and cultural programming, the following happens:

- The manager or leader shows that he/she trusts the person reporting to him/her.
- The manager or leader will interact regularly with this person, listen to inputs given, consider these and share work-related goals to be reached.
- The person on the receiving end will use initiative, be dedicated, go the extra mile to ensure that goals are reached, thereby not letting down the manager or leader.
- This in turn results in the person taking pride in his/her work and the manager or leader giving the person opportunities to develop.

- Business results are achieved and the trust between the person and manager or leader is reaffirmed.
- The manager's or leader's thought process is that he/she was right about this person and this strengthens his/her belief system about this person and the group that this person comes from, for example, "All lean, white females are energetic and good workers."
- The manager or leader will give preference to this group of people when vacancies arise and most likely earmark people with similar backgrounds and characteristics for appointments and promotions.
- The belief system of both the manager and leader, as well as the person reporting to the manager and leader, is reinforced in the workplace.
- This is then also transferred to the social context within South Africa and both will most likely be more amicable to mix socially outside the workplace.

HOW HIGH EXPECTATIONS AND PREJUDICE AFFECT PERFORMANCE

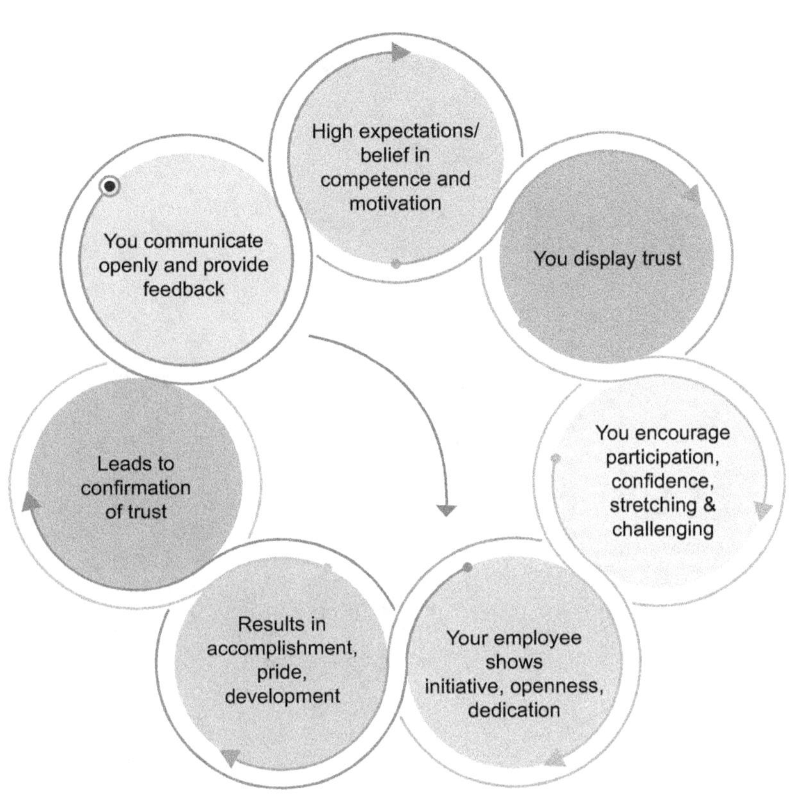

16

LEADING AND MANAGING DIVERSE TEAMS

Being aware of the negative and positive effects of cultural programming, how then does the manager or leader mobilize diverse people to successfully increase productivity in the workplace? Based on the manager's own prejudices if he/she thinks that a person cannot do the job, the following normally transpires:

- Managers and leaders can only succeed if they create awareness for themselves of their ethnocentric beliefs, their prejudices and stereotyping and how this can and will affect their behavior in the workplace.

- Managers and leaders must create a greater understanding of themselves; this is also where emotional intelligence comes in as they must be in tune with their own feelings as well as the feelings of others.

- Managers and leaders must make a concerted effort to develop constructive work relationships with those people who are different from them as well as similar to them.
- Managers and leaders must focus on effective teamwork where all inputs are listened to and considered, not only those from likeminded people who think in similar ways to them.
- The focus should be on increased productivity and customer satisfaction for all team members, no matter how similar or different they are.
- Managers and leaders must set common goals and a common approach for all team members on how to achieve these goals.
- Managers and leaders must use social intelligence or "common sense" to play the political game in the workplace and create a balance between flexibility and consistency, thereby accommodating differences whilst harnessing similarities to achieve greater productivity and improved business results.

Practical tips for managers and leaders that will ensure employees remain engaged and encourage positive actions:

- Spend time listening to people
- Have a positive optimistic attitude about the work and the people in your team
- Point out the things that employees do right instead of just focusing on their mistakes
- Whenever possible, involve employees in decision making, especially about how you as a team can achieve business goals effectively
- Show genuine care for your employees
- Be open-minded towards employees' ideas, especially ideas that are different from yours

- Regularly solicit new ideas from people
- Don't view mistakes as catastrophes
- Create a safe atmosphere for dialogue and open and honest discussions
- Be sensitive to the feelings of people
- Encourage employees to trust you by modeling the way and creating an environment of honesty
- When giving feedback, always do this in a constructive manner – both positive and negative feedback
- Clarify expectations of both acceptable behaviors and performance and confirm that you believe they can achieve this
- Be a positive team leader who communicates that we "can do it"
- Treat everyone equally
- Do not confront people in front of others but do so in a private place where they do not feel degraded
- Have confidence that with proper training, coaching, and mentoring, your employees will be able to do their work effectively
- Develop an ability to see hidden assets and potential
- Value each person who brings a specific strength and skill set to your team
- Focus on mutual co-operation, rather than competition in order to build a powerful team
- Allow people to be themselves and encourage different thoughts
- Recognize and reward behaviors and performance that embrace diversity in your team
- Ensure that all team members understand that, in order for the business to be sustainable, performance of acceptable standards

is not negotiable and that you will always be there to guide and support them to deliver and be successful

17

DIVERSE LEADERSHIP ACROSS CULTURES/GENDERS

Diversity is not limited to South Africa alone and can clearly be seen in the different management and leadership styles internationally. It is interesting to note that nationality alone to a large extent defines the type of leaders and managers that emerge from different countries – mainly due to cultural programming once more!

Let's take a look now at how different leadership styles are found worldwide. If you work for a multinational company in your home country, do not underestimate the diversity impact of the mother company based in another part of the world – this is an additional diversity dimension that managers and leaders must consider and contend with.

- The Dutch culture is an egalitarian society and is skeptical about the value of leadership. Terms like leader and manager carry a stigma. If a father is employed as a manager, Dutch children will not admit it to their schoolmates.

- The Arabs worship their leaders – as long as they are in power!
- The oriental leader is expected to behave in a manner that is humble, modest, and dignified, to speak infrequently and only on critical occasions.
- The Iranians seek power and strength in their leaders.
- The French appreciate two kinds of leader.
  A strong, charismatic leader like De Gaulle, and a consensus builder, coalition former, and effective negotiator like Mitterand.
- The Americans also appreciate two kinds of leader. They seek empowerment from a leader who grants autonomy and delegates with confidence. They also respect the bold, forceful, confident, and risk-taking leader as personified by John Wayne and the robber barons.
- The Japanese culture is based on a system of seniority determined by hierarchical levels. It is seen as impolite to have a major difference with a senior official, as offence would be taken. People engagement is limited and conflict is avoided. Mistakes are not tolerated by leaders and long working hours and years of employment are valued. Leaders instruct and employees follow. Leaders lead through consensus decision-making.
- German leaders can take quick decisions and are egocentric. Differences are heard but must make sense. Leaders are precise and know what they want.

In contrast to these international styles of leadership, South Africa has its own unique leadership style with a diversity aspect. White and black leaders value different focus areas, as is the case between male and female.

In general terms, the White South African Manager/Leader Profile focuses on the following, which is largely influenced by the Western or Eurocentric style of leadership:

- Competition and a work orientation
- Free enterprise
- Liberal democracy
- Materialism
- Individual self-sufficiency
- Self-fulfillment and development
- Exclusivity, planning, methodology, and structure

In general terms, the Black South African Manager/Leader Profile focuses on the following, which is largely influenced by the Afrocentric leadership style of Ubuntu:

- Collective solidarity
- Inclusivity, collaboration, consensus, and group significance
- Concern for people as well as working for the common good
- Structure through rituals and ceremonies, patriarchy, power, respect, and dignity

Given the population mix of South Africa, and other legal interventions such as employment equity and B-BBEE, the workplace going forward will comprise of more and more black people who value an Afrocentric management approach.

Diversity leaders must take cognisance of this fact as the emphasis will be on:

- Group harmony through co-operation, collaboration, consensus, and interdependence.
- Treating all employees with respect and care and allowing them to save face.
- Employee wellbeing and defending their interests.
- Internal promotions based on experience and competence.
- Flexible policies and practices.
- Group decision making and objective incentives.
- Healthy competition.
- Group achievements with joint responsibility.

Just to make it more interesting, another aspect of diversity, namely gender, highlights leadership differences in South Africa.

Male managers and leaders generally tend to focus on:

- Performance
- Competition and winning
- Domination
- Control and Directive Leadership

Female managers and leaders generally tend to focus on:

- Collaboration
- Participation
- Intuition
- Empathy
- Empowerment
- Self-Disclosure
- Subtle forms of control

- Being in tune with their own feelings as well as the feelings of others
- The development of people

18

HOW TO APPRECIATE DIFFERENCES

Managers and leaders in the workplace must actively foster the appreciation of dealing with different people or persons who are different to themselves.

Tips for managers and leaders on how to appreciate differences in the workplace:

- Value it – show people that it's OK to have different opinions and that these are considered.

- Acknowledge it – listen to ideas and traditions that are not similar to yours and be aware of your own prejudices.

- Model it – lead by example and inspire and influence others to do the same.

- Reward it – praise behaviors that support diversity in the workplace and discourage the converse.

- Learn from it – listen attentively to ideas and practices that are different from yours and choose not to socially isolate yourself as a leader.

Managers and leaders must, through their thoughts and behaviors, trust and respect people upfront who are different and similar to themselves, until proven otherwise. This will minimize prejudicial thinking. They must also seek to create understanding of differences in the workplace amongst team members, ensure clear communication on both differences and similarities, and improve their knowledge of people who are different and similar in the workplace – this starts with the managers and leaders and filters down to the team members you manage or lead.

A good example of the above is the sharing of facts about religious and cultural traditions – it will spark a lot of interest and create empathy in the workplace between people. Lose your fear of the unknown and next time when you are invited to the funeral of a black person or wedding of a white person, attend – you will learn a lot!

In this way, trust and respect are reinforced amongst everyone in the workplace. Find creative ways to increase understanding and communication to address matters from different people and groups of people in the workplace, not only those you are accustomed to.

Accept that differences will always be there – embrace this idea and have a positive way of thinking about differences – it's exciting to learn something new; don't create your own barriers to appreciating the strength that differences can bring to your life and to that of the workplace.

As people we are all unique – in our uniqueness lies our strength! We are not copies of one another as that would mean "much more of the same." **Accept this principle and foster it in the workplace.**

HOW TO FOSTER APPRECIATION FOR DIVERSITY

- **Value it** - appreciate the positive effects of diversity
- **Acknowledge it** - encourage acceptance of differences in the workplace
- **Model it** - lead by example and be a champion of diversity
- **Reward it** - recognize success and give recognition
- **Learn from it** - be open minded and listen attentively to other opinions different to yours

---

It is the responsibility of managers and leaders to create a work environment in which different people can reach their full potential and flourish, as this will impact positively on business results.

This is not difficult!

HOW TO CREATE THE RIGHT ENVIRONMENT FOR DIVERSITY

- **Trust** – allow people to have different opinions
- **Respect** – balance consistency with flexibility
- **Understanding** – create a balance between personal differences and business goals
- **Communication** – encourage honest and open communication
- **Knowledge** – gather and share relevant information about diversity matters

---

Managers and leaders who have a diverse workforce will face the challenge of how to get those who are similar and those who are different to cooperate and deliver the required business results.

Trust should be the cornerstone of your success. People generally follow those whom they trust!

HOW TO LEAD A DIVERSE WORKFORCE EFFECTIVELY

The Three Cs

- **Competence** – managers and leaders must be seen as knowledgeable, skilful, and having a positive attitude
- **Communication** – managers and leaders must listen with an open mind to everyone and give honest feedback in a constructive manner. Important decisions must be communicated to all.
- **Care** – show your people that you care for and respect them. Accommodate personal needs where operationally possible. Get to know them!

PART 4

EMBRACING DIVERSITY IN A CHANGING WORLD

19

DIVERSITY IN A CHANGING WORLD

With the new decade in 2020, South African organizations are faced with the 4th Industrial Revolution. The only consistent thing is *change*:

- Change is inevitable
- Change is necessary
- Change is possible
- Change is here

Whilst robots will take over routine tasks and help improve quality assurance and time frame of production lines, work will have to be reorganized, resulting in people requiring new skills to be effective and successful.

There are, however, certain key skills that businesses will require that robots cannot do. This is evident in the identification of the top ten job skills people will need in 2020 and beyond as outlined in the study done by the World Economic Forum, 2020, in its report, "The Future of Jobs."

This study highlights the fact that businesses, despite utilizing robots who do not have a people-centric approach to business success, will not be viable over the long term. The list below from the Future of Jobs study, highlights the importance of new managerial and leadership skills required for success, as well as a clear focus on how important people are for business success. Remember, people are diverse, and some will think and behave like you as a manager and leader. Others will think and behave differently from you due to their own cultural programming. This poses a new dimension to the "Diversity Impact" in the workplace from 2020 onwards. So be ready and prepare for this new challenge!

In his book, *The Principles and Benefits of Change*, Dr. Myles Munroe lists the 10 ways leaders respond to change:
1. Leaders expect change
2. Leaders initiate and create change
3. Leaders interpret change
4. Leaders guide change
5. Leaders plan and design change
6. Leaders prepare themselves for change
7. Leaders are inspired by change
8. Leaders grow through change
9. Leaders benefit from change
10. Leaders exist for change

Managers and leaders will therefore need to develop new skills to manage their current workforce that is already diverse. This is high-lighted by the World Economic Forum's identification of the top ten workplace skills required, as listed below :

1. Complex problem solving – people need to have the mental capability to solve complex problems never encountered before but within a fast-paced changing work environment.

2. Critical thinking – people must be able to use logic and reasoning to consider various options and come up with the correct solution.

3. Creativity – people must be able to connect the dots with information that seems disconnected and come up with novel ideas.

4. People management – managers and leaders must know how to motivate this new workforce, encourage teamwork, and maximize productivity whilst at the same time responding to peoples' needs.

5. Coordinating with others – people must up their game in collaborating with others, which involves strong communication skills.

6. Emotional intelligence –people must be in tune with their own emotions and those of other people.

7. Judgment and decision-making – this will have to be amped up as it will revolve mostly around company data, sifting through information to inform business proposals and strategies.

8. Service orientation – people must be able to anticipate the ever-changing needs of customers and translate them into product offerings, whilst understanding the processes to meet these demands.

9. Negotiation – people will be expected to show greater

interpersonal skills as well as the ability to negotiate with colleagues, teams, managers and leaders, and clients.

10. Cognitive flexibility – people must be able to flex their cognitive ability by learning new things and embracing the unfamiliar.

Robots that will take over routine tasks will increase productivity and accuracy during the 4th Industrial Revolution. Looking at these top ten skills required in the workplace from 2020 onwards, it is clear that people are at the center. As robots infiltrate the workplace, job re-organization will take place and it is clear that robots cannot perform these ten top skills – only diverse people can, or people with different skills who complement each other!

Therefore, managers and leaders need to understand that social skills will be more important than ever before for people in the work-place, as well as the impact thereof on their management and leader-ship skills that should be adapted in order to achieve success.

The challenge for managers and leaders to harness their diverse workforce is to:

- Create a work environment conducive to fostering the top ten workplace skills.
- Recognize and reward these top ten skills.
- Coach and mentor people on how to improve interpersonal and negotiating skills.
- Create a learning environment where critical thinking is strongly encouraged – when people think differently then creative solutions are the result – let different people feed off each other and in this way use diversity as a competitive advantage.

- Encourage and insist on breaking down silos and building strong, independent teams that collaborate with others in the organization.
- Recognize that the unknown is scary and inspire people to face the new world of work with tenacity.
- Lead by example and empower, be flexible and agile, and encourage a positive attitude towards change.

Diversity champions who are astute will also ensure they have developed additional critical leadership skills to ensure their success during the new decade, the fast-changing (new normal) of the 4th Industrial Revolution, and the global effects of COVID-19:

- Cultural adaptability
- International business knowledge
- Innovation
- People wellness
- Time management
- Resilience
- Adaptation and management of change

It is clear from the above that people are the most important resource that organizations will have to retain and to gain a sustainable future. Managers and leaders must realize that people management and social skills must be their priority for business success.

Never underestimate the people focus for business success, and more importantly, be thankful that diverse people in your teams bring strengths, so harness this diversity to your advantage!

20

MANAGEMENT AND LEADERSHIP SKILLS FOR THE NEW DECADE

As discussed in chapter 19, the new job skills required by people reporting to you as a manager or leader will require that you adapt your own leadership skill set and take it to a novel level of competence.

As your team becomes more and more diverse with different generations requiring different things from you as a leader, topped up by robots changing the way things were always done in the workplace, leaders must be agile and able to react to fast-changing needs with resilience.

The new decade from 2020 onwards will require managers and leaders to have a strong interface between intelligence, emotional, and social intelligence if they want to be successful in a fast-paced, changing environment.

A people-centric approach to the 4th Industrial Revolution requires a new set of skills for managers and leaders.

A combination of the following three skills will allow you to champion and lead a diverse workforce as never previously required by managers and leaders:

1. IQ (Intelligence Quotient) – people follow competent people and so a high level of intelligence, cognitive ability, and competence will be required. This, however, is not sufficient to lead people in the 4th Industrial Revolution that is upon us,
   and even technically proficient managers will have to develop the skills discussed in points 2 and 3 that follow in order to be successful.

2. EQ (Emotional Intelligence) – managers and leaders must be able to understand and identify their own emotions as well as the emotions of others. You must be emotionally aware and be able to apply these emotions to processes such as problem-solving and creative thinking. In order to encourage effective teamwork and collaboration in a diverse workforce you must be able to help others control their feelings whilst at the same time having control of your own.

3. SQ (Social Intelligence) – managers and leaders who interact with a wide variety of people must be able to use appropriate and tactful words whilst playing different social roles and being aware of the unwritten rules of engagement or "workplace politics." This is a key skill for managers and leaders to assist in fostering appreciation for diversity in the workplace.

The interface between being competent as a manager and leader, whilst being emotionally aware and socially in tune with others will allow your team to embrace you as a leader, foster innovation, and create an environment of "It's okay to be myself and different as I bring different strengths to the team, whilst at the same time strengthening the teams resilience to change and allowing the team to focus on future goals and business results."

Competent managers and leaders with a high level of social and emotional intelligence will be able to get the most out of their teams that are diverse by building constructive working relationships with each person and the team as a whole and then getting the team to be future-focused to achieve business results. This is because of the integrated new skill set of intelligence, emotional understanding, and social awareness. All three are essential for embracing innovation and managing people who will effectively become more and more diverse.

Managers and leaders will be able to:
- Use socially expressiveness to be tactful with a wide array of people.
- Be aware of unwritten rules of social interaction and use common sense and be street smart in navigating their paths in the workplace.
- Listen well to different people and embrace different opinions and viewpoints.
- Understand what makes people tick by paying attention to how people behave and what they say.

Late management expert, Peter Drucker, said, *"The purpose of an organization is to enable ordinary people to achieve extraordinary things."*

The drastic changes brought about by the 4th Industrial Revolution makes it clear that a new skill set will be required by both diverse employees as well as managers and leaders. It is incumbent upon managers and leaders to upgrade their own skill set by integrating intelligence, emotional and social intelligence to be agile in and flexible to a new world of work, whilst fostering an environment that encourages and embraces diversity.

Utilizing the strength that diversity brings to the workplace will make it easier for managers and leaders to develop the top 10 key skills required for business success in the new decade 2020 onwards. In order to be effective, managers and leaders must:

- Effectively manage their own image as a leader that they portray to others – be politically and socially astute
- Understand how their interactions with others impact on them
- Control their own feelings and emotions, thereby minimizing conflict in the workplace
- Read the emotions of others, as well as their body language, enabling them to be proactive in their own reactions
- Tap into their social intelligence so they can focus on the best way forward to achieve the best results for the business

21

LESSONS LEARNT

From 2020 onwards a new decade in the world of work has dawned upon us all. The impact of the 4th Industrial Revolution and the reorganization of work will shine the spotlight on the importance of a people-centric business approach to creating business sustainability.

This people-centric business approach will be more challenging than ever before as new people-related skills are required. Moreover, the impact of diversity will become more and more important in the workplace and will require a new level of managerial and leadership skills.

Besides the known dimensions or elements of diversity, the workplace 2020 onwards will have more elements of diversity. Sexual orientation and age are two such elements. Managers and leaders will face the challenge of aligning different personal needs with business needs and having five different generations working together in one work-place.

The lessons learnt to date are invaluable and more lessons will be learnt as the decade unfolds and the diversity impact is felt and seen in the workplace:

1. Unity does not mean conformity.
2. Diversity is not sameness.
3. Be an original of yourself not a copy of someone else.
4. Diversity brings strength not weakness.
5. Diversity enables a higher level of creativity and problem solving.
6. Be aware of your own feelings of superiority, as this impacts on others.
7. We have all been culturally programmed.
8. Fundamentally we all, no matter how different, want the same things.
9. Recognize that people are a source of competitive business advantage.
10. Everyone must break loose from the shackles of the past.
11. It is your choice to embrace diversity and make a difference.
12. It is okay to associate with people similar to you.
13. It is empowering to associate with people different from you.
14. Have a positive attitude about diversity.
15. Differences in people is nothing new and has always been there.
16. Create your own awareness of how your cultural programming influences your behavior, decisions, and attitudes towards others.
17. Be careful that your thinking is not distorted, resulting in prejudice, bias, stereotyping, and discrimination.

18. Make a concerted effort to get to know those in the workplace who are different from you – you will learn a lot!

19. Encourage and create teams of diverse people as they are "stronger together" due to diversity impact.

20. Create common business goals and a common business approach to unify differences.

21. Create a work environment of trust, respect, and understanding of differences.

22. Feel free to raise valid opinions about work-related issues without fear of being different.

23. Be careful not to let your own prejudices influence your expectations, low and high, of those who are different or similar to yourself – this is dangerous!

24. All people, no matter how different, must conform to and meet company standards, behaviors, and goals.

25. Different nationalities working together brings its own set of diversity challenges.

26. Different people will trust managers and leaders who are competent, communicate well, and show they care for others.

27. Managers and leaders must be fearless and lead a diverse workforce with agility, empowerment, and integrity.

28. Give all people the opportunity to develop and grow, and do not limit opportunities to a select few.

29. Balance and integrate intelligence, emotional, and social intelligence in order to embrace innovation, encourage teamwork, and minimize conflict in the workplace.

30. It is not so important where you come from but where you are going!

31. Do not see diversity as a threat but rather an asset.

32. The strength of a diverse workforce, much like culture, will impact the organization negatively or positively.

33. Diversity is therefore a management and leadership challenge in the new decade 2020 onwards.

34. Diversity is not a temporary fix – it is permanent.

35. Learn to see color and other visible differences so that you can consciously accommodate diversity.

36. When interacting with people, do not focus on changing a person but rather the person's behavior.

37. Solidarity requires diversity.

38. Differences allow the accomplishment of greater things.

39. Harness uniqueness to achieve business results.

40. The creator, God, is the authentic author of diversity.

41. Workplace and personal journeys in life are taken together with other people – some similar to you and others different from you.

42. People are purposely made differently so they can complement one another.

43. A Venda Proverb says, *"Wa sa tshimbila u do mala khaladzi"* – if you don't travel to meet diverse people, you will end up marrying your sister. Not a good road to take!

44. Personal growth in life is from the places you go and the people you meet.

45. Get out of the comfort zone where your happiness lies but where there is no growth.

Some interesting quotes of different leaders to consider:

AFRICAN

Former South African president, Nelson Mandela, said, *"For to be free is not merely to cast off one's chains, but to live in a way that respects and enhances the freedom of others."*

Mandela, in his book, *Long Walk to Freedom,* said, *"No one is born hating another person because of the color of his skin, or his background, or his religion. People must learn to hate, and if they can learn to hate, they can be taught to love, for love comes more naturally to the human heart than its opposite."*

A proverb of Muslim origin says, *"A lot of different flowers make a bouquet."*

Former South African Anglican Archbishop, Desmond Tutu, says, *"Isn't it amazing that we are all made in God's image and yet there is so much diversity amongst his people."*

South African minister, Dr Elijah Maswanganyi, said, *"All cultures are unique, good, bad, dynamic, and sinful."*

"Diversity is the one true thing we all have in common. Celebrate it everyday!" (Author unknown).

The TshiVenda proverb, *"Zwanda zwi a tanzwana"* (one hand washes the other), expresses the idea that mutual cooperation can help both parties. It is similar to other proverbs like, *"One good turn deserves another"* and *"You scratch my back and I'll scratch yours."*

An African proverb says, *"If you want to go fast, go alone; if you want to go further, go with others."*

International

Performing artist, Phil Collins, says, *"Deep inside we are not that different at all."*

Former U.S. president, Jimmy Carter, said, *"We have become not a melting pot but a beautiful mosaic. Different people have different beliefs, yearnings, hopes, and dreams."*

International leadership expert, Dr. Myles Munroe, said, *"We are products of our culture, and interpret the world based on our conditioning."* He also said, *"Every human being is born with a seed of greatness."*

American Entrepreneur, Malcolm Forbes, said, *"Diversity is the art of thinking independently together."*

An old Chinese proverb says, *"If you want prosperity for one year, grow grain, for ten years, grow trees, and for a hundred years, grow people."*

22

EMBRACE OUR DIFFERENCES

As representivity levels slowly start to change in organizations, and disadvantaged individuals become managers and leaders, they too must be aware of their own cultural programming in order to break the cycle of the past. The "Irish coffee" syndrome will in time become one of a "chocolate milkshake." The taste will become distinctly different but will in the new decade become an acquired taste for everyone.

As the coronavirus pandemic increases in South Africa, so does the fear of the unknown as neither a treatment nor a vaccine is available yet. The new echelon of managers and leaders in the new decade in the workplace must allay the fears of an ever-increasing diverse workforce.

People in the workplace must realize they require new skills for the business to be successful. People who are similar and different must

127

pool these skills together to achieve empowered teamwork and reach business goals. "Together we are stronger," as each person brings a different set of skills to the table.

The real challenge for managers and leaders is to focus on the building of agility and resilience in the workplace. This can only be achieved through people – those who are similar to you as well as those who are different from you. Embrace differences and allow people to be themselves. People need an environment where they can remain real and not be forced to change their identity for others. Managers and leaders must appreciate and accept differences in the workplace and create a positive environment where people can be empowered and thrive.

The coronavirus has shown that all South Africans can experience solidarity in the face of a common enemy. Managers and leaders in the workplace must inspire and influence all people to focus on the achievement of business results with a common approach through true leadership and a high level of emotional and social intelligence.

The impact of the coronavirus could be devastating for South Africa but due to the inclusive leadership style of our State President, South Africa is commended by the World Health Organization for the manner in which the situation has been handled. Similarly, the impact that diversity in this new world of work, with its new challenges, could have on business results depends largely on how managers and leaders utilize the strength that diversity brings to companies.

ABOUT THE AUTHORS

Mr Charlie Masala

Born in the village of Manamani in Venda, South Africa, Charlie Masala is a Management Consultant, Speaker, Trainer, and Facilitator who is full of brilliant insight, human interest, and passion. He was personally mentored by the late leadership expert, Dr. Myles Munroe. Charlie speaks on a broad spectrum of topics such as Diversity Management, Leadership in Transforming Societies & Organizations, Teamwork/Team Building, Building Organizational Brands, Mentorship, Employment Equity, Discovering Your Purpose, Recruitment, Labor Relations, Entrepreneurship, Youth Leadership Development, and Leading Change. As a Human Resources Generalist, Charlie served corporate South Africa for over 12 years before venturing out on his own as a Management Consultant and Conference Speaker.

Charlie is a dynamic international speaker and has spoken at top organizations such as Sasol, Barloworld, Development Bank of Southern Africa, South African Bureau of Standards (SABS), ABSA Bank, National Youth Development Agency (NYDA), SASOL, International Training College, Holland, Tshwane University of Technology, HP (Hewlett Packard), and several South African government departments and municipalities. Charlie's presentations provide audiences with tools to change their lives for the better and his witty presentation style has won him accolades from these top organizations.

Charlie holds a National Diploma in Human Resources (Tshwane University of Technology), Labor Relations Management Specialist Certificate (IPM), Leading Change Program (University of Michigan Business School), Management Development Program (University of Pretoria), and Thabo Mbeki African Leadership Programs offered through University of South Africa (UNISA).

Charlie's career started at the Council for Scientific and Industrial Research (CSIR), and thereafter he worked at the Office of the Auditor General SA, Integrated Labor Solutions, and as Human Resources & Development Manager at African Bank Limited.

Charlie founded and served as Managing Director of ZOE Business Consulting, National Director of Macedonia International Bible Fellowship (MIBF), Senior Vice President of International Third World Leaders Association (ITWLA), Board Member of The Myles & Ruth Munroe Foundation, and CEO of Myles Munroe International–Africa (Munroe Global).

In his role as speaker, trainer, strategist, organizer, and management consultant, Charlie has traveled to over 40 countries around the world, capacitating leaders and organizations. Visit charliemasala.com or email: charliemasala@icloud.com.

Ms Gail Vermeulen

Gail is a Master HR Professional (MHRP) registered at the South African Board for People Practices (SABPP).

Gail holds a Masters degree in Labor Law and a Honors Degree in Strategic Human Resource Management and Labor Relations. She has also lectured in Human Resource Management at different institutions in South Africa.

She has extensive experience spanning more than 30 years at senior/executive management level in various industries in the corporate world, including multinational companies in South Africa. Gail also successfully run her own Human Resources/Industrial Relations Consultancy. She has assisted different companies in the private and public sectors to transform their workplaces using practical change management programs, such as the design and facilitation of leadership development programs, graduate development programs, organizational restructuring, and the facilitation of strategy sessions, to mention just a few.

Whilst leading large and diverse Human Resource teams, Gail was always tasked to take on the role of Transformation Manager. She has trained thousands of South Africans on diversity championing, employment equity, performance, and talent management. She has also put into place employee engagement structures to facilitate greater understanding of different viewpoints and goals to achieve business success. This includes unions, contractors, employers, and other social partners such as community engagements.

Gail has received international recognition for HR Leadership from the World Sustainability Congress, hosted by the World Human Resource Development Council (WHRDC). In 2015, this accolade was bestowed on her for HR Leadership in Africa, and in 2019, for HR Leadership in South Africa.

Gail's personal background has set the tone for her to strive to be the best version of herself that she could possibly be, and her motto is "move out of your comfort zone where there is happiness but no growth." Gail can be contacted on gvermuelenconsultancy@outlook.com.